Young Offenders and Alcohol-Related Crime

A Practitioner's Guidebook

Mary McMurran

Rampton Hospital, Nottinghamshire and
The University of Birmingham, UK

Clive R. Hollin

Youth Treatment Service and
The University of Birmingham, UK

JOHN WILEY & SONS

Chichester · New York · Brisbane · Toronto · Singapore

Other Wiley Editorial Offices

John Wiley & Sons, Inc., 605 Third Avenue,
New York, NY 10158-0012, USA

Jacaranda Wiley Ltd, G.P.O. Box 859, Brisbane,
Queensland 4001, Australia

John Wiley & Sons (Canada) Ltd, 22 Worcester Road,
Rexdale, Ontario M9W 1L1, Canada

John Wiley & Sons (SEA) Pte Ltd, 37 Jalan Pemimpin #05-04,
Block B, Union Industrial Building, Singapore 2057

British Library Cataloguing in Publication Data

A catalogue record for this book is available from the British Library

ISBN 0-471-93839-4 (paper)

Typeset in 10/12 Century Schoolbook by
Mathematical Composition Setters Ltd, Salisbury, Wiltshire.
Printed and bound in Great Britain by Biddles Ltd, Guildford, Surrey

Young Offenders
and Alcohol-Related
Crime

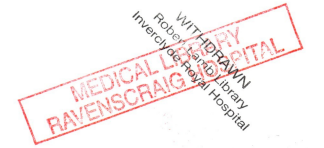

MM: To my parents, Mary and George McMurran, with love.

CH: For my mum, who never touches a drop.

Contents

Series Preface

Twenty years ago it is doubtful that any serious consideration would have been given to publishing a series of books on the topic of offender rehabilitation. While the notion of rehabilitation for offenders was widely accepted 30 years ago, the 1970s saw the collapse of what we might call the treatment ideal. As many other commentators have noted, the turning point can be pinpointed to the publication of an article titled "What Works—Questions and Answers about Prison Reform", written by Robert Martinson and published in 1974. The essential message taken from this article was that, when it comes to the rehabilitation of offenders, what works is "nothing works". It would be stretching the case to say that Martinson single-handedly overturned the rehabilitative philosophy, but his message was obviously welcomed by a receptive audience. As writers such as Don Andrews have suggested there are many reasons why both the academic community and politicians and policy-makers were more than willing to subscribe to the "nothing works" philosophy. (Although the evidence suggests that the public at large did not buy completely the need to abandon rehabilitation.) Thus the 1970s and 1980s saw a return to hard sentencing, the predominance of punishment, and the handing out of just deserts to those who transgressed the law of the land. Throughout this period of rehabilitative nihilism a small group of academics and practitioners kept faith with the rehabilitative ideal, led perhaps by Paul Gendreau and Robert Ross, and slowly began to look for new ways to argue the case for rehabilitation. The turnabout, when it came, was dramatic. Through the development of a methodology for statistically reviewing large bodies of research, called "meta-analysis", unequivocal evidence was produced that rehabilitative programmes did work. The view that "nothing works" is simply wrong: rehabilitation programmes do have a positive effect in reducing recidivism. The effect is not always large, although sometimes it is; nor is it always present, although on average it is. However, it is there and that cannot be ignored. Since 1990, armed with these findings, there has been a remarkable resurgence of the rehabilitative ideal: practitioners have eagerly attended conferences, seminars, and training courses; researchers are working not to make the case for rehabilitation, but to improve and refine techniques for working with offenders.

This series aims to provide a ready source of information, for both practitioners and researchers, on the developments as the renewed emphasis on rehabilitative work with offenders gathers pace. We are keenly looking forward to its unfolding, and we hope that in time practitioners and researchers will also eagerly await each new volume.

Mary McMurran
Clive R. Hollin

October 1992

Preface

We met each other 13 years ago at the outset of our work with young offenders. At that time, we were both prison psychologists working in Borstals. Over the years, we saw the Borstal sentence give way to Youth Custody, and then to detention in a Young Offender Institution. Although sentencing policy changed, the offenders themselves did not. All along we saw that a large percentage of young offenders in institutions came there as a consequence of offences committed in relation to drinking. Colleagues in the Probation Service assured us that a similar situation pertained in community-based work with offenders: they too were challenged by alcohol-related crime.

Over the years, in both our research and practice, we have addressed issues relating to young offenders and their drinking. The knowledge and experience we have gained forms the basis of this book. The format in which the book is presented owes much to the training courses we have prepared for staff from a variety of disciplines: probation officers, prison officers, prison psychologists, nurses, residential care staff, social workers, and alcohol counsellors. It is for professionals such as these that this book is intended.

The text provides the background, evidence, and methodology for conducting interventions with young offenders to reduce both their drinking and drink-related crime. These interventions may be used equally well in secure settings and in the community, and are appropriate for both young men and young women. The age range of the offender population to whom the interventions apply is probably wider than that suggested by legal definitions of a "young" offender, particularly at the older end of the continuum. Professionals can consider using this book to guide their work with offenders who are in their twenties or thirties.

Thirteen years on, we are both still involved in work with young offenders, although we have also developed other aspects of our professional lives. We see this book as a summary of our work so far, and not the final statement. Indeed, we hope that our readers will be encouraged to develop services for young offenders with alcohol-related problems, evaluate the outcome of their interventions, and report their findings in professional and academic journals. Only by such efforts will our knowledge and skills be gradually advanced.

We would like to express our gratitude to those who helped us with this book: Stephen Rollnick, whose suggestions were so helpful; Wendy Hudlass at John Wiley & Sons, who provided timely, and gentle, reminders; and Tracey Swaffer and Rebecca Howarth, for help in compiling the references.

Mary McMurran
Clive R. Hollin
August 1992

Chapter 1

Young Offenders and Drinking

The aim of this opening chapter is threefold: to define our use of the term "young offender"; to review briefly the role of alcohol in the offending of young people; and to discuss the merits of interventions with young offenders who drink. We begin therefore with a search for a definition: what exactly is a "young offender"?

JUVENILE OFFENDING

One approach to defining criminal behaviour generally is to take a legal standpoint: Williams (1975) offers the view that "A crime is an act that is capable of being followed by criminal proceedings". This definition immediately raises two important points:

1. to be a *criminal* act, that act must be so defined by criminal law;
2. the individual who commits the act must be capable of being dealt with under criminal law.

The first point leads to the important distinction between anti-social behaviour and criminal behaviour: the former is not necessarily the same as the latter. For example, it is generally agreed that burglary is an anti-social act and this is reflected in criminal law; it might equally well be felt that, say, computer fraud is an anti-social act, but this is altogether less clearly defined in criminal law. Such discrepancies between what might generally be considered anti-social and what is defined in criminal law reflect changes in society. In the recent past, acts such as abortion and certain homosexual acts have been removed from the criminal law domain; other changes have made it illegal to sell certain solvents to children. There are acts such as those noted above that pass in and out of criminal law; there are, however, other acts which are almost universally judged to be "bad in themselves". Such acts include those which inflict harm on another person, for example, assault and rape; or which interfere with another person's property, such as malicious damage or theft.

These points allow us to arrive at the first part of our working definition of young offender: a young offender is a young person who has committed an act that is "capable of being dealt with by criminal proceedings". This explicitly excludes "anti-social behaviour" of any other sort such as non-compliance with parental demands and disruptive behaviour in school. This latter type of behaviour is best thought of as "conduct disordered" and hence is held apart from criminal behaviour.

The second definitional point referred to above relates to whether an individual is capable of being dealt with according to criminal law. There are several reasons why, despite having committed an act defined as criminal by law, criminal proceedings may not follow. The perpetrator may be too young to be held legally responsible for his or her actions and so cannot be tried under criminal law. The age of criminal responsibility varies from country to country but is typically about 10 years of age. (Similarly, the distinction between "young" and "adult" offenders varies, but it is generally set at around 18 years of age.)

The diagnosis of mental disorder is another reason for not progressing with criminal proceedings. As with age, different legal systems have different definitions of mental disorder, although the term can generally be taken to include those diagnosed as mentally ill, usually with schizophrenia and depression; those with psychopathic disorder; and those with significant mental impairment. The mentally disordered young offender poses treatment issues that are beyond the range of this book.

Taking the force brought to bear by these latter points, we can arrive at a more precise definition of "young offender" for our present purpose: *A young offender is a person within legally prescribed age limits, not suffering from mental disorder, who commits an act capable of being followed by criminal proceedings.*

The word "capable" is an important one: the young person does not actually have to be caught to be an offender; technically it is enough that the act is committed for the young person to be deemed a criminal.

What Types of Offences do Young People Commit?

First of all, is offending an unusual form of behaviour among young people? With adolescent populations the distinction can be drawn between *status* offences and *index* or (*notifiable*) offences. Status offences are those acts that apply only to adolescents and not to adults: these offences include, for example, under-age drinking, under-age driving, and truancy. Index offences, by contrast, are serious offences regardless of the age of the perpetrator: this category therefore includes offences such as burglary, theft, and assault. Young people do, of course, commit both types of offence, but in what numbers?

How Many Young People are Involved in Crime?

In truth this is an impossible question to answer: there is a gap of unknown size between official figures and undetected crime, something that is termed the "Dark Figure" by criminologists. Nonetheless, if we consider both status and index offences, the research suggests that very high numbers of adolescents become involved in crime. Indeed, estimates in excess of 80% of the adolescent population are not uncommon. Farrington (1987) suggests that if unrecorded offences were to be included with the official figures, this would "undoubtedly push those figures close to 100 per cent" (p. 34). However, Farrington goes on to suggest that most offenders do not commit serious index offences.

About 30% of criminals apprehended for serious crimes are juveniles; most adolescents on the other hand actually commit relatively trivial status offences. This is illustrated in a study reported by West (1982) that looked at offending among a sample of 405 14-year-old boys. West found relatively high rates for minor offences such as breaking windows in derelict property (68.9%), but much lower rates for more serious offences such as using weapons in fights (12.1%).

Over the past five years or so a number of longitudinal studies have been conducted, both in England (Farrington & West, 1990) and America (Wolfgang, Thornberry & Figlio, 1987), that have presented some revealing data concerning age and crime. Farrington (1983), reviewing offending from 10 to 25 years of age, arrived at four conclusions: (1) The peak age for most offences is 16—17 years; (2) juvenile and adult crime are closely related; (3) as the number of convictions increases beyond six or more, so the probability of further convictions becomes greater; (4) juveniles convicted at the earliest ages (10—12 years) become the most persistent offenders.

The first finding, that offending peaks at around 16—17 years of age, suggests that there is a "life span" to most delinquent activity. As Farrington (1986) notes: "Typically the crime rate increases from the minimum age of criminal responsibility to reach a peak in the teenage years; it then declines, at first quickly, but gradually more slowly" (p. 189).

Importantly, it appears that the peak in offending is caused by a rise in *prevalence* rather than *incidence*. In other words, the rise in adolescent offending is caused by more non-offenders committing offences, rather than by existing offenders committing more offences as they grow older. Wolfgang *et al.* (1987) are in agreement with this point, noting the consistency of the number of offences per offender, which varied from an average of 1.2 to 1.8 offences per year. They conclude that the peak in offending at around 16—17 years of age "is due almost entirely to an increase in the number of active offenders and not to an increase in their annual 'productivity'" (p. 44).

It can be stated with some confidence that most young people will, at some time in their early life, commit a criminal act. However, only a very small number of these criminal acts culminate in a court appearance, with the type and seriousness of the act being major determinants of a court appearance. Crimes such as car theft, serious assault, and breaking and entering are much more likely to end in a court appearance than petty vandalism and minor theft (West & Farrington, 1977). It is those adolescents in the former group who go to court and become "official young offenders".

A number of studies have addressed the issue of whether "official young offenders" differ in any important way from the general population of "unofficial young offenders" who never appear before the courts. The most obvious distinguishing characteristic is the seriousness of the offence: as noted above, most offences are trivial and it follows that only a minority of young people are "at risk" of legal intervention because of their criminal activity. It is also likely to be the case that the amount, as well as the seriousness, of offending by convicted young offenders is greater than that of non-apprehended young offenders.

The differences, however, extend beyond the number and seriousness of the criminal acts. As shown in Table 1.1, West (1982) reported a range of individual, family, social, and economic differences between persisting recidivists, temporary recidivists, and non-offenders. It is also known that those apprehended and prosecuted early in their

Table 1.1 The primary adverse features associated with young offenders (after West, 1982)

1. "Troublesome" at primary school
2. Low family income
3. Large family size
4. Criminal parent
5. Unsatisfactory child rearing
6. Lower quartile of IQ

criminal careers are significantly more likely to be criminals as adults. In summarising the position with regard to official and unofficial young offenders, Rutter and Giller (1983) are concise and to the point: "The view that everyone is somewhat delinquent and that there are no meaningful differences between those who are slightly so and those who are markedly so can be firmly rejected" (p. 29).

It is important to add as a final note here that Rutter and Giller (1983) are not stating that differences of the type noted in Table 1.1 are necessarily the cause of criminal behaviour. The relationship between offender characteristics, the legal system, and economic, social and political systems is too complex to allow such an inference to be made. Indeed, the study of such complex relationships between these economic, social, political, and individual factors in large part defines the discipline of criminology (Siegal, 1986), within which psychology has made its own contribution (Hollin, 1989).

DRINKING AND DELINQUENCY

Drinking Patterns and Problems

Before looking specifically at drinking and delinquency it is worthwhile to set this topic in context. In this country, drinking alcohol is a pastime followed by the large majority. Estimates from population censuses show that in excess of 90% of the populace drink on at least an occasional basis. It is true to say that for most of those who enjoy an occasional drink alcohol is a social lubricant, oiling the wheels of successful social intercourse and having little more detrimental effect than an annual hangover on the 1 January. However, it is also the case that alcohol can be taken to excess, affecting the individual whose drinking becomes out of control, members of his or her social network, and members of society generally. Excessive drinking is one of the factors most consistently associated with physical and mental health problems; with absenteeism from work; with suicide; with family violence and family disharmony and breakdown; with traffic accidents and fatalities; and with crime.

While, of course, high levels of alcohol consumption can be found in all strata of society, epidemiological research has clearly shown that excessive drinking is more likely to be found among some parts of the population than others. A survey carried out in Great Britain by Goddard and Ikin (1989) showed that 18–24 year old men drank appreciably more than other groups. With a unit of measurement where 1 unit is equal to 1 standard drink (i.e. 8 grammes of alcohol),

Goddard and Ikin found that the 18—24 year old males reported an average consumption of 21.4 units per week. This represents, in other words, an average weekly intake of about 10 pints of beer or lager. This level of drinking just exceeds the "safe" limit (for men) of 21 units per week recommended by the Royal College of Physicians (1987).

If we look to a younger adolescent group we see that high alcohol consumption has been a cause for concern for a number of years (Glatt & Mills, 1968). While not reaching the same levels as for the 18—24 year old males, there is ample evidence to suggest that 13—17 year olds are drinking significant amounts of alcohol. For example, a study by Marsh, Dobbs & White (1986) showed that 13-year-olds had a mean weekly intake of 8.3 units, rising to 16.1 units in 17-year-olds. It goes without saying that it is highly unlikely that these are "safe" levels given the differences in physical maturity and physiological functioning between adolescents and adults.

Studies of the relationship between alcohol consumption and personal problems in young people show, not surprisingly, that heavier drinkers report more problems. In this light, an American survey of young people's drinking reported by Werch, Gorman & Marty (1987) provides some interesting findings. Werch *et al.* found that as alcohol consumption increased so did the number of alcohol-related problems; however, specific types of problem became evident with different levels of drinking. Light drinkers experienced physical discomforts such as hangovers, nausea, and vomiting; moderate drinkers showed more school and social problems; heavy drinkers were more likely to run into trouble with the police. This pattern seems to suggest a developmental pattern: when young people start to drink they have a low tolerance for alcohol and therefore experience the physical effects of drinking; if, however, drinking becomes established then social and legal problems begin to develop. Given this, the study of alcohol consumption among delinquents has been of interest to a number of researchers.

Young Offenders and their Drinking

It is true to say that the study of alcohol and crime is not solely concerned with young offenders: there is a substantial empirical and theoretical literature on alcohol and criminal behaviour that concerns itself with all age groups (e.g. Collins, 1982). However, for present purposes we shall concentrate on young offenders.

One of the first problems faced by researchers in this area is to disentangle the conceptual knots between cause and effect. For example, popular mythology holds a relationship between alcohol and crimes of violence, as witnessed by the recent "lager lout" scare. However, if we consider the empirical evidence (not just for young offenders) then a rather different picture emerges:

> Evidence does not establish that people who drink commit crimes nor does it prove that those who commit violent crimes drink to excess. It does reveal how often one is intoxicated when caught in the act of committing a crime. This is problematic if the very act of being intoxicated increases the probability of being apprehended (Murdoch, Pihl & Ross, 1990, p. 1067).

Again this serves to set the context for what follows: the findings noted below are from studies conducted with convicted young offender populations and, taking the point made by Murdoch *et al.*, we are aware of the limitations of these data. Therefore, we are not making a theoretical statement regarding the nature of the relationship between alcohol and criminal behaviour, but rather stating the extent of the problem for a sample of the young offender population.

West and Farrington (1977) found that from a sample of young people judged to be "heavy drinkers" a high proportion committed delinquent acts. Sleap (1977) recorded an average weekly consumption of 84.05 units among a sample of convicted young offenders in an English penal institution, suggesting a "problem drinker" rate of 40% among the young offenders. Similarly, Fuller (1979) recorded a rate of 30% problem drinkers at a young offender establishment in Wales; while Heather (1981; 1982) found that 27% of a sample of young offenders received into a Scottish young offender institution were classified as either dependent on alcohol or problem drinkers. Hollin (1983) suggested that 15% of a sample drawn from an English young offender institution were either dependent upon alcohol or heavy drinkers; a further 26% were "at risk". McMurran and Hollin (1989a) found that a sample of young offenders, again from an English institution, reported drinking an average of 58.15 units of alcohol per week. Such a level of alcohol consumption is not only far in excess of a "safe" level of 21 units, it is well above the level of 49 units per week that the Royal College of Physicians suggests is *dangerous* for men (and probably more so for adolescents).

Clearly, there are those among young offender populations who drink to excess, but what relationship does this have with their offending? In several of the studies noted above the young offenders were asked if they perceived any relationship between their drinking and their offending. For example, Hollin (1983) found that 39% of his sample said that they thought their drinking and delinquency were related to each other. However, there was no difference for property and person offenders; this point was later emphasised by Welte and Miller (1987) who argued that alcohol does not play a different role in the genesis of different crimes. McMurran and Hollin (1989a) conducted a study that attempted to look in more detail at the relationship between alcohol consumption and criminal behaviour in young people. This research found that most young offenders were of the view that alcohol directly influenced their behaviour: in other words, drinking led them to do things they would not do when sober. Whether or not this is a convenient excuse or reflects a real phenomenon remains a matter for debate. As well as the effects of alcohol, the social context of drinking was frequently cited as leading to crime. Meeting and drinking with friends was often given as the beginning of a train of social exchanges culminating in offending. However, drinking was sometimes a consequence rather than an antecedent of delinquency: a number of young offenders said they drank *after* their offence, either as celebration or to relieve guilt and anxiety. Finally, a substantial number of young offenders said that while they drank heavily this was not connected in any way with their criminal activities. While this research raises as many, if not more, questions than it answers, it does illustrate the complexity of the relationship between drink and delinquency.

To summarise thus far, it is plain that substantial numbers of adolescents drink alcohol in quantity, and that this pattern is to be seen among adolescents who commit crimes. However, the exact nature of the relationship between drinking and delinquency is unclear. Given this, is there a case to be made for intervention with young offenders who drink to excess?

Reasons for Intervention

There are two, sometimes overlapping, reasons for intervention with young offenders who drink: the first rests on the basis of delivery of health care services; the second on the basis of crime prevention.

Health care. If a young person has a personal difficulty to resolve, and wishes to participate in an intervention programme, then the argument can be made that intervention is justifiable on health care grounds alone. The response to such an argument, encountered at some time by most of us who work with young offenders, is that young offenders do not deserve health care initiatives, almost as if their offending disqualifies them from services that should be available to all members of society. We would respond to this view by suggesting that if one considers the backgrounds of many young offenders they will be seen to come from disadvantaged conditions, characterised for example by low income, parental harshness, and poor education. Although they have inflicted pain and suffering on victims, many convicted young offenders are themselves victims of social inequality and sometimes personal abuse. Indeed, one might arrive at the moral position that because of these disadvantages young offenders should be of priority in the delivery of health care services. Further, the delivery of services to young offenders does not mean that the victim of the crime should be forgotten: we are in total support of initiatives for victim support. We simply see no good reason why services for victims and offenders should be at each other's expense.

A recent statement issued by the Committee on Adolescence of the American Academy of Pediatrics (Editorial, 1989) reinforces our views on health care for young offenders. This statement sets out the health care provisions needed by young people held in custody, and offers guidelines as to the contents needed for a comprehensive health care programme. The statement makes the point that:

> It is clear that all citizens, including incarcerated youths, have the right to appropriate health care and that good health care can contribute to the rehabilitation of troubled young people. (Editorial, p. 1120.)

Crime prevention. As discussed previously, in some cases drinking is causally related to offending. The case can therefore be advanced that reducing alcohol consumption may well lead to a reduction in offending. Specifically, this is likely to be the case in the following situations:

> (a) drinking is the crime (for example underage drinking, drunk and disorderly, driving whilst intoxicated); (b) drinking changes behaviour, with offences committed when drunk that would not be committed when sober; (c) drinking has consequences which lead to crime (for example overspending on drink leading to the need to steal); and (d) crime is committed to facilitate drinking (for example stealing alcohol or stealing money to buy alcohol) (McMurran, 1991a, p. 249).

If successful programmes can be devised and run, then the benefits are considerable: fewer victims of crime, advantages for both the offender and his or her family and friends, and less burden on the criminal justice system, saving both time and money.

A note of caution. It would be unwise to confuse the goal of health care with that of crime prevention, which is a perennial issue in working with offenders (Hollin & Henderson, 1984). It is important to state at the outset that the delivery of programmes for problem drinking to young offenders is not guaranteed to reduce criminal behaviour. In certain cases it might well have this effect, most probably with offences where the drinking is the crime, but careful assessment would need to be made in advance of delivery of the programme if crime prevention was the avowed aim (see Chapter 6).

In total we know from various surveys of young offender populations that substantial numbers recognise that they have a drink problem and would be receptive to help with this problem (Hollin, 1983; McMurran & Hollin, 1989a). We also know that great strides have been made in treatment initiatives for drink problems. The problem is: how do we put these two together?

How to Use This Book

This book is intended for professionals of all disciplines who work with young offenders to reduce the likelihood of alcohol-related crime. The material presented here may be used by those working in the community as well as those working in institutions, and applies to both young men and young women. Chapter 2 sets the scene by presenting the basis for a psychological approach to understanding behaviour. Chapter 3 addresses the issue of matching clients with interventions: what works with whom? Based on a stage-of-change model, a modular programme is suggested where clients may be allocated to the appropriate module of the programme and progress to the next module, either to complete the entire programme or exit at a suitable stage. These modules are: Alcohol Education; Motivational Interviewing; Assessment; Behavioural Self-Control Training; Social Skills Training; Relapse Prevention; and Lifestyle Modification. The chapters in this book follow the modules in sequence. In conclusion, Chapter 11 highlights the importance of evaluation.

Chapter 2

Understanding Behaviour

Social responses to drinking and drunkenness are not fixed or static: they vary from one culture to another and within any culture they vary across time. Interventions to reduce alcohol consumption are shaped by the beliefs and attitudes prevalent in any place at a particular time. In this chapter, a brief summary of the history of responses to excessive drinking will be presented as a background to the understanding of the range of interventions currently in existence. Since the interventions described in this book are based primarily upon psychological models of behaviour, basic concepts will be described more fully.

Responses to Excessive Drinking: a Brief History

Excessive drinking has been construed in a variety of ways over time. In 18th century Britain and America, drinking alcohol, even in large quantities, was socially acceptable. Drunkenness was viewed as a social nuisance and punishments were meted out to offenders by magistrates and civil authorities (Heather & Robertson, 1985).

In the 19th century, attitudes to drinking and drunkenness changed. The development of more censorious attitudes to drinking is usually attributed to the industrialisation of society: where drinking by agricultural labourers was not considered to be detrimental to work performance, the same could not be said for workers operating machinery. Alongside the Industrial Revolution, developments in science and medicine were also occurring. One significant development was the application of scientific concepts and methods to explain human behaviour. This set the scene for the first constructions of excessive drinking as a disease, first stated by Benjamin Rush, an American physician, in 1785.

These two developments—the industrialisation of society and the emergence of the disease model of alcoholism—formed the foundations on which the Temperance Movement was built. Adherents of the Temperance Movement promoted teetotalism for the greater social good, using the disease model of alcoholism in support of their case. Religious groups, particularly Protestant denominations, gave weight to the Temperance Movement which gained in strength, and in America in 1919 the ultimate success was achieved—Prohibition.

Prohibition was an amendment to the Constitution banning the production, sale and transportation of intoxicating liquors for beverage purposes. Fingarette (1989) described Prohibition as impossible to implement, provoking a malevolent form of nationwide gangsterism, although successful in reducing overall alcohol consumption and related health problems. The fervour of the Temperance Movement gradually waned and public opinion turned against Prohibition, making it politically untenable. Prohibition was repealed in 1933.

After the repeal of Prohibition in America, the prevalence of drinking problems increased, yet further attempts at legislative control would have been politically disastrous for any Government. Against this background, an apparently scientific approach to problem drinking was an almost inevitable development and the disease model of alcoholism grew in strength. Private agencies, basing their programmes on the ideology of the Alcoholics Anonymous (AA) movement, began to dominate the field of treatment. In 1960, Jellinek cautiously expressed an hypothesis that some, but not all, heavy drinking may be the symptom of a disease in which the drug ethanol changes cell metabolism to produce craving and loss of control. This hypothesis, usually interpreted as fact, lent authority to the AA ideology.

The disease model of alcoholism rests on the following three premises:

- that alcoholics experience craving and loss of control
- that craving and loss of control result from biological abnormalities
- that these abnormalities are irreversible and, although the disease of alcoholism cannot be cured, it may be arrested through abstinence.

The central premises of the disease model—craving, loss of control, and irreversibility—have repeatedly been exposed as flawed. In 1962, Davies reported a return to normal drinking in 7 of 93 former alcoholics who had been treated for alcohol addiction between 7 and 11 years previously. This report created some controversy, with critics suggesting that those drinking normally had never been true alcoholics, or were not now genuinely normal drinkers, or were in the process of relapsing to alcoholism, or were biochemical "freaks"

(Heather & Robertson, 1981). A similar controversy surrounded the publication of the Rand Report in 1976 (Armor, Polich & Stambul, 1976). A follow-up study of a sample of people treated in a number of American Alcoholism Treatment Centers suggested not only that controlled drinking was a sustainable option for some, but that fewer erstwhile alcoholics who achieved controlled drinking relapsed to heavy drinking than did abstainers. This report was unjustifiably criticised as methodologically unsound and ethically unprincipled (see Armor, Polich & Stambul, 1978).

In addition to the observation that former alcoholics could drink normally, the concepts of craving and loss of control were discredited in experimental investigations. Merry (1966) gave alcoholics an orange vitamin drink, in some cases laced undetectably with vodka and in some cases not, and then asked all subjects to rate the strength of their craving for alcohol: he found no differences between those given alcohol and those not given alcohol. Marlatt, Demming and Reid (1973), in a balanced placebo design, gave problem drinkers either vodka and tonic or plain tonic whilst telling half of each group that they were drinking alcohol and the other half that they were drinking a soft drink. Subjects were then invited to drink as much as they wished, supposedly to form opinions about brand preferences. Those who were told that they were drinking alcohol drank most, irrespective of whether their drinks actually contained alcohol or not. Marlatt, Demming and Reid (1973) explained their results in terms of a cognitive rather than a biological basis for apparent loss of control.

Finally, Sobell and Sobell (1973; 1976) and their colleagues (Caddy, Addington & Perkins, 1978) compared the outcome over three years of a number of alcoholic men allocated to a goal of either abstinence or moderation in either a behaviourally based intervention or traditional AA group therapy. The main findings were that a controlled drinking outcome could be achieved and that the behaviourally based intervention was superior.

With the demise of the disease model of alcoholism, psychological models of drinking have gained strength, and controlled drinking has become a more widely accepted goal of intervention. Within a psychological framework, drinking may be construed as a learned behaviour, with classical conditioning, operant learning, instruction and modelling each playing a part. In a such a model, a wide range of factors, both external and internal to the individual, are understood to set the scene for drinking to occur (antecedents) and the effects of drinking for the individual (consequences) determine whether and at what level drinking re-occurs. This model is represented diagrammatically in Table 2.1.

Table 2.1 The socio-psychological model of drinking

Antecedents	Behaviour	Consequences
Cultural		Positive reinforcement e.g. social rewards; mood enhancement
Familial		Negative reinforcement e.g. avoid boredom; relief of withdrawal symptoms
Social		
Situational	→ Drinking →	
Cognitive		Positive punishment e.g. hangovers; crime
Emotional		Negative punishment e.g. fail to sustain relationships; fail to find employment
Physiological		

The advantages in a model based on learning theory are that all drinking behaviour should be explicable, not just problem drinking; the designation of problem drinking is not dependent on a single cut-off point, but depends on individual experiences; problematic drinking patterns, since they are learned, may also be unlearned; and abstinence, although sometimes advisable, is not a necessary goal. Taking this approach, it is clear that, irrespective of alcohol consumption levels, where an individual experiences an alcohol-related problem, whether physical, psychological, or social, an intervention could be provided: thus services should no longer be reserved only for chronic heavy drinkers. Since the interventions described in this book derive mainly from learning theories, some basic issues will be covered in more detail.

PSYCHOLOGICAL MODELS OF BEHAVIOUR

The search for an understanding of the causes of behaviour has a long history steeped in the tradition of looking *inside* the person to explain *outward* behaviour. The emphasis on an inner world is evident in biological theories, from which the medical model derives, but also in psychological theories. This is true of the theories of Sigmund Freud, undoubtedly the most widely known and influential of psychological theorists.

The essence of Freud's position is that our observable actions are the result of a continual, dynamic interaction of inner forces. These inner forces, which Freud said were psychological in nature but biological in origin, were conceived as an intricate psychodynamic system, operating at both conscious and unconscious levels. Freud's ideas proved a rich source of inspiration for following generations and there are several post-Freudian schools offering variations on Freud's original theories (Brown, 1961; Kline, 1984).

Classical Conditioning

The beginning of a very different approach to explaining behaviour occurred around the turn of this century in the laboratories of the Russian physiologist and Nobel prize winner, Ivan Pavlov. Pavlov's research was concerned with an investigation of the canine digestive system, and it was while engaged in this work that Pavlov made a significant observation. He saw that dogs who were accustomed to the laboratory salivated not only at the sight or smell of food, as would be expected, but also to cues related to the presence of food, such as the clanking sound of the food pails. Hungry dogs salivate naturally to the sight or smell of food, but why should they salivate to the noise of clanking pails? The answer, as Pavlov discovered, is to be found in the phenomenon of learning by association: certain environmental events, such as particular sights or sounds, become associated over time with a naturally occurring reflex response, such as salivation, so that artificially they are able to elicit the reflex response. In Pavlov's laboratory, the dogs had learned an association between a certain sound and the arrival of food, so that the sound of the approaching food elicited the salivation even if no food was forthcoming. This process of learning by association is called *classical conditioning*.

Pavlov's work is of historical importance because it heralded the notion that behaviour could be explained through interaction between the person (or animal) and the outside world. In other words, rather than behaviour being seen as the product of some biological or psychological force *inside* the person, an alternative understanding of the world was born with an emphasis on events *external* to the person. This idea was to revolutionise the discipline of psychology as researchers began to see behaviour as a phenomenon worthy of study in its own right, rather than a by-product of mysterious inner forces.

The founder of this new behavioural approach was the American psychologist, John B. Watson, whose 1913 paper "Psychology as the behaviourist views it", caught the mood of the times in an American university system ill at ease with the prevailing unscientific, mentalistic, European approaches. Simply, Watson argued that humans, like other animals, are born with various innate stimulus—response reflexes—the grasp reflex, the eye blink reflex, the suckle reflex, and so on. Through classical conditioning, building on these innate reflexes, Watson argued, we learn ever more complex sequences of behaviour. The task of psychology was to develop, scientifically, an understanding of learning, so discovering the laws by which behaviour could be predicted and changed.

With the benefit of almost 80 years of research and debate, we now know that the acquisition and development of behaviour is too complex to be reduced to chains of association stemming from innate reflexes. In one sense this does not matter, since it is the line of thought initiated by Watson and the ensuing 80 years of research which are important. Pavlov and Watson, like Freud, had set into motion a new way of thinking about the world, and in the same way that Freud's ideas were developed by the post-Freudians, so Watson's ideas have been developed by the neobehaviourists. This is not to say that classical conditioning should be dismissed; on the contrary, it still has an important part to play in the explanation of behaviour (Rescorla, 1988). However, additional explanations are needed to account for the richness of learning.

The individual destined to be the greatest of the neobehaviourists was a psychologist working at Harvard University who, between 1930 and 1935, developed the basic concepts for a new approach to understanding behaviour. This new approach was called *behaviour analysis* and its proponent was the American psychologist B. F. Skinner.

Behaviour Analysis

As Kazdin (1979) noted, one of the great mistakes in many texts is to dismiss behaviour analysis as simplistic and mechanistic. While the principles of behaviour analysis may be readily understandable, the philosophical and theoretical issues are complex and taxing. It is beyond the scope of this book to discuss the philosophical and theoretical implications of radical behaviourism, and any reader who wishes to grapple with the complexities should refer to recent books by Catania and Harnad (1988), Hayes (1989), Lee (1988), Modgil and Modgil (1987), and Zuriff (1985).

The basis for Skinner's contribution can be traced to a line of research, perhaps most often associated with Edward Thorndike, an American psychologist working in the early 1900s, concerned with the relationship between the outcome of a behaviour and the probability of that same behaviour recurring in the future. Skinner's research was an attempt to understand the relationship between a behaviour and its consequences. As was the fashion in the 1920s and 1930s, Skinner's early studies were carried out with rats, pigeons, and squirrels. In a typical study, the animal would be placed in a closed box—now known as a Skinner Box—and its behaviour carefully observed and recorded. The use of a closed environment such as a box allows the researcher to control events and so see exactly their effect on behaviour.

When placed in a Skinner Box the animal, say a rat, will explore its new environment. One of the features of a Skinner Box is a bar, and when the rat approaches the bar the researcher arranges for food to be delivered into a tray inside the box. After eating, the rat will return to the bar and explore further, eventually placing its front paws on the bar; with a click, the bar drops down and food is automatically delivered into the tray. The rat will quickly learn that its behaviour, the bar press, can operate on the environment to produce a certain consequence, which in this case is delivery of food, although there could be other consequences, such as delivery of drink, or access to other rats. This type of behaviour—that which operates on the environment to produce specific consequences—Skinner termed *operant* behaviour, and hence this type of learning is called *operant learning*. The relationship between behaviour and its consequences is called a *contingency*, and Skinner formulated the principles of two important types of contingency, which he named *reinforcement* and *punishment*.

Reinforcement

A reinforcement contingency is present when consequences of a behaviour *increase* the likelihood of that behaviour occurring in the future. There are two types of reinforcement contingency—positive reinforcement and negative reinforcement. *Positive* reinforcement takes place when behaviour is either maintained or increased by producing consequences which the person (or animal) finds rewarding. *Negative* reinforcement, on the other hand, occurs when the behaviour produces the consequence of avoiding or escaping from an aversive situation.

While signifying an important advance in understanding behaviour, these principles also form the basis for strategies to change behaviour. Suppose a parent wishes to increase an adolescent's compliance with instructions to come home at a reasonable hour: the goal of increasing behaviour means that a reinforcement strategy is required. The parent has to decide between using rewards or aversive control: compliance might be made contingent on a pleasant outcome, such as praise or a tangible reward; alternatively, failure to comply might be made contingent on some aversive outcome, such as loss of a privilege or pocket money. While both strategies will increase the targeted behaviour, assuming accurate identification of a reinforcer, the first uses positive reinforcement and the second uses negative reinforcement. The above example shows how these are very different in practice and how they will be perceived differently by parent and adolescent.

The point made above concerning the accurate identification of reinforcers is important: it is easy to assume that the same things are rewarding for everyone, for example money or praise, but this is not the case. Some people, perhaps adolescents in particular, find praise far from rewarding (Brophy, 1981). Conversely, what might be seen by most people as unrewarding or even aversive, such as verbal or physical abuse, can in certain situations act as a reward for some people, and so reinforce behaviour.

Punishment

The term "punishment" as used in behaviour analysis has a different meaning from that of its everyday usage. A punishment contingency is the opposite of a reinforcement contingency in that the consequences of a behaviour lead to a *decrease* in the frequency of that behaviour. As with reinforcement, there are two types of punishment, sometimes termed positive and negative punishment, which can be used to change behaviour. Suppose a parent is faced with an adolescent who drinks excessively, a behaviour which the parent wishes to suppress or, in operant terms, punish. The parent has a choice of two strategies: the drinking can be made contingent upon the delivery of some aversive outcome, such as extra work around the house, or the drinking can be followed by the loss of a privilege, such as withdrawal of permission to go out at the weekend. In the former instance, an unpleasant outcome is made contingent on the behaviour, which is positive punishment; in the latter case, the loss of a reward is negative punishment. As with reinforcement, the choice of strategy is only punishing if it leads to a decrease in behaviour.

It is important to emphasise that in the way it is used by behaviour analysts, the term punishment refers to a particular relationship between a behaviour and its consequences; it does *not* mean the infliction of physical pain or highly distressing events.

Three-term Contingency

Having considered behaviour and its consequences, there is one more factor to discuss in order to complete this brief introduction to behaviour analysis. Behaviour, in the main, does not happen at random; environmental cues signal that if a certain behaviour is carried out it is likely to be reinforced or punished. For example, an adolescent may be more likely to break a parental rule by drinking at a party when previously told not to where a number of cues—such as the presence of friends, the availability of alcohol, and the freedom from adult supervision—will prompt the drinking. The adolescent has learned that drinking in the presence of these cues produces either rewarding outcomes, such as peer approval (positive reinforcement), or a reduced likelihood of other outcomes, such as feeling socially uncomfortable (negative reinforcement). The relationship between the setting or antecedent events, the behaviour, and the consequences is called a *three-term contingency*. This gives rise to the much used A:B:C format—Antecedent : Behaviour : Consequence—which is the essence of behaviour analysis.

Functional Analysis of Behaviour

The goal in conducting a behavioural analysis is to come to an understanding of a behaviour through the formulation of an A:B:C analysis for a given behaviour. In essence, the goal is to understand the *function* of a behaviour for the individual in terms of reinforcement and punishment, hence A:B:C analysis is properly referred to as a *functional analysis*. A useful distinction to make is that between assessment and analysis: the former is the gathering of data and information; the latter is the process of making sense of this information. More about assessment and functional analysis will be found in Chapter 6.

While it is historically true that the principles of behaviour analysis were formulated with studies in animals (often referred to as the *experimental* analysis of behaviour), the task of *applied* behaviour analysis is to use these principles to understand human behaviour. The movement away from the laboratory and the controlled environment of the Skinner Box into the real world makes this an immensely difficult task. The difficulties are twofold: the complexity of most people's lives makes it impossible to discover every event in their learning history; and people differ from animals in a number of important ways which demand adjustments in the principles derived from

animal studies. The principal differences which have to be accommo-
dated are people's cognitive abilities, use of verbal language, and the
nature of our social environment. In addition, our understanding of
the place of human factors in behaviour analysis is constantly
changing as research progresses (see, for example, Lowe, 1983). These
difficulties imply that the completeness of a functional analysis will
always be limited and that the formulation of a functional analysis
depends on the skill and ability of the analyst; the process cannot be
reduced to rigid, mechanical formulae. Nonetheless, applied behaviour
analysis can be used to develop an understanding of all social
behaviours from the "micro" level of an individual to the "macro" level
of a culture (Lamal, 1991; Skinner 1986a).

The "Problem" of Private Events

In seeking to establish a scientific basis for the emerging discipline of
psychology, Watson argued that because the private world inside the
skin is impossible to study scientifically it should not be of concern to
the psychologist. One of the unfortunate legacies of Watson's
behaviourism is the criticism that behaviourism denies the existence
of, or at best ignores, "private" events such as thoughts and feelings.
Such a criticism is entirely misplaced if directed at contemporary
behaviourism: indeed, as Skinner (1974) stated: "A science of behaviour must consider the place of private stimuli. . . . The question, then,
is this: What is inside the skin and how do we know about it? The
answer is, I believe, the heart of radical behaviourism" (pp. 211—212).
In part answer to his own question, Skinner (1986b) has suggested the
place of private events as follows: "In a given episode the environment
acts upon the organism, something happens inside, the organism then
acts upon the environment, and certain consequences follow" (p. 716).

The key issue which arises, and which is the crux of the "problem",
is whether what happens inside the skin can be considered as behaviour, and hence be part of behaviour analysis, or whether internal
events should be accorded a separate status, perhaps mentalistic or
spiritualistic, and so fall outside the realm of behaviour analysis. The
position of applied behaviour analysts is that private events are
behaviours and therefore can be understood within the terms of
behaviour analysis; that is, private events are seen as being
established by a particular environment and they are maintained and
modified by environmental consequences.

Do private events *cause* behaviour? Again, Skinner is clear: "Private events . . . may be called causes, but not initiating causes"
(Catania & Harnad, 1988, p. 486). The initiation of behaviour,

including private behaviour, is to be found in the environment, most often our social world. However, once initiated, one behaviour can lead to another and so on, thus private behaviour can act as the stimulation for overt, observable behaviour. For example, if another car bumps into your car, then you might become angry and shout (or worse!); from the point of view of applied behavioural analysis, you shouted not because you were hurt and angry, although pain and emotion were undoubtedly involved, but because initially the environment acted on you to initiate a sequence of reactions that culiminated in your verbal behaviour. Your behaviour (remembering that behaviour includes private events) will produce environmental consequences which, the next time your car is bumped, will either reinforce or punish the chain of behaviours that culminated in your shouting on this occasion.

The practical or technical difficulty lies in the assessment of private events. By definition, private events are not observable and so we must rely on self-report to find out about them: the problems then are with the accuracy and reliability of self-reported information. Self-report can be unreliable for a number of reasons: the person may want to withhold the truth; the very act of self-observation can change the nature and functioning of the private event; and some private events may take place outside awareness, as when dreaming, and so are not amenable to self-observation. It may be that these problems will be overcome in time; at present, however, we must work within the limitations. More information about self-report is given in Chapter 6.

Social Learning Theory

Of course, not all theorists agree with applied behaviour analysis and there are a number of other important psychological theories. *Social learning theory* is in part an extension of operant principles, but with changes in the role and status of cognition (Bandura, 1977a; 1986). In operant theory, behaviour is initiated and reinforced by the environment; social learning theory, however, uses the concept of motivation rather than reinforcement. Motivation can take three forms: *external reinforcement*, as in operant learning; *vicarious reinforcement*, which comes from observing the rewards contingent upon the behaviour of other people; and *self-reinforcement*, as in a sense of pride or achievement. While social learning theory retains some overlap with behaviour analysis, the introduction of motivation as a cause of behaviour, as well as the concepts of internal and external reinforcement, marks a clear divergence from applied behaviour analysis.

Integration

The theoretical research and debate continues apace and, as theories advance, so do treatment styles and methods (Fishman, Rotgers & Franks, 1988). In a little more than two decades, behaviour modification has been supplemented by cognitive—behaviour modification, followed by the rise of cognitive therapy (Brewin, 1988). The integration of the various cognitive—behavioural approaches in relation to drinking behaviour is summarised in a recent report by the American Institute of Medicine (Committee to Identify Research Opportunities in the Prevention and Treatment of Alcohol-Related Problems, 1992), as follows:

> The central assumptions of the social learning perspective predict multiple pathways to alcohol use. They propose that alcohol use/abuse and alcohol-related behaviour are learned within a cultural context and superimposed on an individual's biologically determined predisposition to problems with alcohol, if any. One major part of this approach that sets it apart from many others is that the individual is viewed as an active agent in the learning process; thus, persons who have learned to misuse or abuse alcohol can also learn self-regulation of alcohol use. Specific cognitive information-processing mechanisms—an individual's beliefs, expectations, coping skills, and perceptions of self-efficacy— play a central role in regulating alcohol-related behaviour. Understanding these mechanisms is essential for developing effective prevention programmes. (p. 7.)

Summary

Responses to drinking and drunkenness vary across cultures and over time, depending on the social and scientific beliefs which prevail. Particular attention has been paid in this chapter to psychological models based on learning theories, namely classical conditioning, behaviour analysis, and social learning theory. These theories are not specific to drinking behaviour, but rather they apply to all behaviours. Nor are they specific to "abnormal" behaviours, but rather they apply to the complete range of possibilities, in this case total abstinence from alcohol through to persistent excessive drinking.

The concept of functional analysis of behaviour has been introduced. This is the method whereby information gathered during assessment about the antecedents (setting events), behaviour, and its consequences is integrated in such a way as to explain the acquisition and maintenance of an individual's behaviour. The next step is to identify appropriate interventions and this is the subject of the following chapter.

Chapter 3

Matching Clients with Interventions

An historical account of the ways drinking and problem drinking have been construed in the Western world provides an understanding of the menu of goals and interventions that exists today. Amongst this range of interventions, there is no single superior approach which is equally effective with all individuals; the issue of matching clients with interventions to maximise the likelihood of successful outcomes is therefore an important one. The essence of matching is captured in the question "what interventions work best with which clients?" In this chapter, the range of available interventions will be described and discussed in relation to appropriateness for use with young offenders. Methods of matching young offenders with specific interventions will be provided.

THE RANGE OF INTERVENTIONS

Four major models of excessive drinking have prevailed over time. These models are: (1) the moral model; (2) the temperance model; (3) the disease model; and (4) the learning model.

The Moral Model

The moral model emphasises personal choice in drinking, and drunkenness is seen as a sin or as wilful misconduct. When the emphasis is spiritual, the intervention is religious persuasion conducted by the clergy or lay representatives of the religious community. When the emphasis is social misconduct, the intervention is punishment by law enforcement agencies.

The Temperance Model

The temperance model holds alcohol as a substance hazardous to personal and social well-being and the intervention is enforced moderation through legislative controls, for example, control of cost, availability, and advertising, and by educating people about the disadvantages of excessive drinking.

The Disease Model

The disease model suggests that some people have an inherent biological predisposition to alcoholism and that these people must abstain in order to hold the disease in check. Alcoholics are treated by doctors or by recovering alcoholics.

The Learning Model

The learning model explains drinking in terms of a combination of classical, operant and social learning. Maladaptive drinking, since learned, can be unlearned. The relevant interventions are within the professional domain of behaviour therapists.

A variety of interventions has been derived from these models; these are listed in Table 3.1.

Table 3.1   The 4-model range of interventions

Model	Interventions
Moral	Punishment Religious persuasion
Temperance	Education Legislative controls
Disease	Drug therapy Detoxification and rehabilitation Alcoholics Anonymous
Learning	Aversion therapy Cue exposure Behavioural self-control training Social skills training Relapse prevention Lifestyle modification

Proponents of each of these models have typically argued the superiority of their particular approach whilst dismissing others as misguided and ineffective. The truth is that no single approach to helping people with drinking problems is markedly superior to all the rest. However, within the wide range of possible interventions there are specific types of intervention which will not be addressed in this book. These are listed below, along with reasons for their exclusion.

Legislative Controls

The drinking environment may be controlled through legislation, for example, pricing policies, licencing laws, and codes of advertising practice. Although these issues are important, they are beyond the scope of this book. For further information, readers are referred to Tether and Robinson's (1986) book "Preventing Alcohol Problems: A Guide to Local Action".

Punishment

Attempts to prevent alcohol-related crime through punishment and deterrence may be seen as essential in that they signal society's attitudes as to what constitutes reasonable behaviour and they protect society from the worst consequences of alcohol abuse (Home Office, 1987). However, as Ross and Lightfoot (1985) point out, whilst criminal sanctions may be seen as an essential response to alcohol-related crime, they may not be a sufficient response. The law operates to control behaviour through the potential offender's understanding of the risks and penalties associated with unlawful acts, yet after drinking alcohol a person's judgments of these risks will be impaired. Therefore, whilst applying criminal sanctions may be important, these need to be augmented by effective programmes which help offenders modify their behaviour.

Religious Persuasion

A revival of religious interest is a common response to the search for meaning that a period of imprisonment often precipitates. Pastoral counselling draws upon both the behavioural sciences and theology to help people cope with their problems. Counsellors who take this spiritual approach will find the interventions described in this book useful, but should refer to other sources for information about the relevance of religion. "Basic Types of Pastoral Care and Counselling" by Howard Clinebell (1984) provides a useful overview.

Drug Therapy

There are two classes of drug used in the treatment of alcohol-related problems. The first is the antidipsotropics, such as disulfiram, commonly known by its trade name Antabuse, which create an adverse physical reaction when alcohol is consumed. The second is the psychotropics, such as anti-depressants or anti-anxiety drugs, which are used to treat underlying psychopathology.

Miller and Hester (1986a; 1986b), in their reviews of treatments for alcohol abuse, concluded that antidipsotropics can be effective, particularly with older, socially stable men with a long history of alcohol-related problems. This suggests that young offenders are not amongst those for whom these drugs are helpful. In addition, Miller and Hester pointed out that antidipsotropics have side-effects which are damaging to health and so questioned the wisdom of their use as a therapeutic agent.

With regard to psychotropic drugs, Miller and Hester (1986a; 1986b) suggested that these do not produce reliable changes in drinking behaviour. Indeed, many problems concurrent with alcohol use will remit once the drinking problem has been resolved; psychotropic medication, therefore, may be most appropriately administered when psychopathology persists during after-care. Whilst some young offenders may require drug treatments for psychiatric problems, addressing the alcohol problem first should in fact clarify the need for such treatment.

Detoxification and Rehabilitation

Some people who are severely dependent on alcohol will experience withdrawal symptoms upon abstinence, and inability to cope with these symptoms may act as a barrier to their stopping drinking. Detoxification is a procedure supervised by a doctor, conducted on either an out-patient or an in-patient basis, involving monitoring of physical state, drug treatment, vitamin administration, and treatment of any arising complicating conditions (Edwards, 1987). Whilst detoxification addresses initial withdrawal symptoms, it is not in itself sufficient for maintaining change and should be supported by rehabilitation. Interventions described in this book will be useful in rehabilitation.

Aversion Therapy

Aversion therapy is where alcohol ingestion is paired with an unpleasant experience, commonly a noxious chemical or an electric shock, to induce a negative response. Miller and Hester (1986a), in their review of aversive procedures, concluded that these may indeed have potential for suppressing drinking behaviour. However, there are difficult ethical and legal issues surrounding aversion therapy, particularly when used with offenders in care, supervision, or custody. Given the availability of effective alternative methods, it is wise to avoid aversion therapy.

Alcoholics Anonymous (AA)

It is no surprise that success in AA is predicted by attendance, that is, people who go along regularly to meetings are likely to benefit from this self-help approach. The typical AA member is male, over 40 years of age, white, middle class, and socially stable (Ogborne & Glaser, 1981). Young offenders often express a lack of affiliation with this group and a consequent reluctance to attend. The AA approach may, therefore, be one that is generally inappropriate for young offenders; however, if a client wishes to join AA, then contact should be facilitated.

MATCHING CLIENT TO INTERVENTION

Although a number of intervention approaches have been excluded as beyond the scope of this book or inappropriate for young offenders, there still remains a number of interventions to which clients must be matched. The matching hypothesis is based on the principles that some people fare better in one type of intervention than in others, and that if clients are appropriately matched to interventions they are likely to show better outcome than those who are simply given whatever is on offer.

Miller and Hester (1987; p. 11) capture the principles of matching in three key statements:

1. There is no single superior approach to treatment for all individuals;
2. Different individuals respond best to different treatment approaches;
3. It is possible to match individuals to optimal treatments thereby increasing treatment effectiveness and efficiency.

The matching hypothesis raises questions about how clients and interventions can be matched to maximise the likelihood of successful outcomes. Information about the process of change provides a useful basis for matching clients with interventions.

Stages of Change

Prochaska and DiClemente (1986) describe a comprehensive model of change in addictive behaviours which can help in matching clients with appropriate interventions. They have identified four well-defined stages of change which form a predictable route from the position of not recognising a problem, through recognition and change, to the point at which the problem no longer exists. These four stages are outlined below.

Precontemplation

People in this stage may be unaware of or unconcerned by their behaviour and its consequences. Precontemplators are unlikely to seek help of their own volition, although they may enter programmes if they are sent by the courts or if they feel coerced by significant others.

Contemplation

In the contemplation stage, a person will recognise some of the negative effects of the behaviour and the benefits of introducing change. However, there is ambivalence since the positive effects of the behaviour are salient and there may be fear of the negative consequences of making a change.

Action

At some point, the motivational balance may tip in the direction of overall negative consequences of the behaviour and a commitment to change will be made. This may be due to a crisis precipitated by the behaviour, or to environmental changes which prevent comfortable maintenance of the behaviour. Young offenders who have attempted to control their drinking without professional help report crime and violence as the main factors in precipitating decisions to stop or cut down (McMurran & Whitman, 1990). The person will now act to effect change.

Maintenance

When a person has consolidated the behaviour change over a period

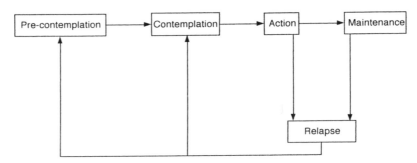

Figure 3.1 The stages of change model (after Prochaska & DiClemente, 1986)

of time, he or she has entered the maintenance stage, which should be the ultimate aim.

Many people do not succeed in their first attempt to change and may revert to their previous behaviour pattern. Relapse is an event that terminates the action or maintenance stage and precipitates return to the pre-contemplation or contemplation stage. The stages of change process is represented diagrammatically in Figure 3.1. This cyclical process may be repeated, often more than once, before the successful maintenance of change.

The stages of change model is of practical value in that it indicates the type of intervention appropriate for an individual in any of these stages, as shown in Table 3.2. Assessment of a client's stage of change will be described later in this chapter. The stages of change model also

Table 3.2 Interventions appropriate at each stage of change

Stage of change	Features	Interventions
Pre-contemplation	Lack of concern about drinking	Education
Contemplation	Considering stopping or cutting down	Motivational interviewing Assessment and feedback
Action	Making active attempts to stop or cut down	Behavioural self-control training (BSCT) Social skills training
Maintenance	Attempting to maintain change	Relapse prevention Lifestyle modification

addresses issues of what type of intervention is appropriate for clients at various stages in the process of change. What it does not indicate are the appropriate goals of intervention, the style of intervention, and the intensity of intervention. These three issues will be examined with reference to young offenders.

GOALS OF INTERVENTION

In aiming to change alcohol consumption and alcohol-related crime, there are two relevant areas to consider: (1) level of alcohol consumption, and (2) pattern of drinking.

Level of Alcohol Consumption

Goals for change in levels of consumption will certainly involve cutting down on previous drinking. The question is, cut down to what level? Clearly, this may range from reduction by a few units of alcohol per week to total abstinence. Research shows that moderation is best achieved by younger people who are less severely dependent on alcohol; have fewer alcohol-related problems; whose problems are of a shorter duration; and who do not regard themselves as alcoholics (Miller, 1983a). This suggests that young offenders are appropriate candidates for reduced drinking goals. However, total abstinence from alcohol may be appropriate for some young offenders, particularly those whose physical health may be at risk from continued drinking, those who have tried to moderate their alcohol consumption in the past but repeatedly failed, and those who choose abstinence as their preferred goal.

Pattern of Drinking

Whilst offending may be related in some cases to levels of alcohol consumption, it may equally be related to the pattern of drinking, that is, the place and time of drinking may create a risk for offending to occur. For example, it is apparent that violent crime is a problem on weekend nights in city centre areas near licensed premises after pubs and clubs close (Hope, 1985; Ramsay, 1982). In such cases, goals might be to reduce levels of consumption on weekend nights, but also to change drinking venues, choose different drinking partners, or alter habits such as time of departure from pubs and clubs and leaving early to avoid the melée.

STYLE OF INTERVENTION

Individual Versus Group Interventions

Interventions conducted one-to-one allow maximum flexibility in addressing an individual's particular problems, yet high levels of demand for services combined with limited resources often lead the professional into group work. Whilst group interventions can present advantages, they must be planned carefully so that young offenders are engaged in the intervention. Issues of selection are important in successful group work: the aims of the group should be clearly defined and group members selected appropriately. Where one or more of the group members are resistant to the professional's aims, they may prove to be the more persuasive force and act to reinforce heavy drinking and crime.

In groups, all members should be of comparable intellectual ability so that they can engage in the discussion and exercises. Individual interventions may be best for those who are unable to keep up with a group programme. In addition, some offenders may have problems which could be exacerbated in a group, for example known sexual offenders may not be accepted by their peers, and individual interventions should also be considered in such circumstances.

In a survey of group work conducted with imprisoned offenders, the typical group size was eight or nine members with two tutors (McMurran & Baldwin, 1989). Although group size does vary, this seems to be generally accepted as an ideal balance, allowing each person the space to contribute whilst having enough people to stimulate discussion and participate in exercises.

Location

Adolescent drinkers are those who are less academically inclined (Jessor & Jessor, 1975), and there is also a significant link between delinquency and truancy (Herbert, 1987). Therefore, adolescents in general and adolescent offenders in particular are unlikely to feel enthusiastic about classroom-based learning and so interventions should be removed from the classroom. The real life context of bars and clubs or even a simulated bar would provide a more stimulating learning environment and there are several additional advantages in working in such a setting. Firstly, in conducting skills training in a naturalistic setting the skills learned may be more likely to generalise to real-life situations. Secondly, the use of cue exposure techniques becomes possible. That is, clients can be exposed to some of the cues that normally trigger drinking (sights, sounds, and smells) without drinking occurring, thus weakening the association between being in a bar and drinking alcohol, and strengthening resistance to temptation (Hodgson, 1989). Thirdly, within a naturalistic setting it may be possible to use alcohol in skills training, thus increasing the ability to apply strategies for controlling drinking after consuming alcohol. At present, sober people are taught skills that they need to apply after a few drinks and it may be more effective to teach clients these skills when they are in the state they will be in when they are expected to apply them.

The use of a simulated bar in interventions to reduce alcohol-consumption has yet to be investigated, although such a facility has been built in one English Young Offender Institution. Such a facility will not be available to most professionals and opportunities for working in actual bars may be limited. Nevertheless, attention must be paid to the environment in which interventions occur, and at very least a comfortable, informal room with the provision of some props for skills training should be arranged.

Tutors

Adolescents typically do not listen to what adults tell them and, where drinking is concerned, adolescents are receiving a "do as I say not as I do" message from adults. In addition, peer pressure to drink is frequently assumed to be one of the most influential controlling factors in adolescent drinking. Therefore, it has been suggested that peer pressure could be used positively by training adolescents to become educators and counsellors for their peers (Swadi & Zeitlin, 1988). Many of the techniques described in this book could be used by young offenders in peer counselling, particularly behavioural self-control training (BSCT) and social skills training. Clearly, this requires proper training and supervision of young offenders identified as suitable peer counsellors.

INTENSITY OF INTERVENTION

Looking at the range of intervention options presented in Table 3.2, these may be understood to lie on a continuum. Some people may respond sufficiently well to advice, whereas others may require a broad-based intervention to tackle their problems successfully.

Advice alone has been shown to be effective. Edwards and his colleagues (1977) found that a brief advice session with problem drinkers was as effective in reducing alcohol consumption at one year follow-up as a more intensive programme comprising behavioural self-control training, problem solving skills training, marital therapy, and psychotherapy. Miller and Sovereign (1989) offered assessment and feedback as part of a health check-up to media-recruited problem drinkers. Over three sessions, volunteers were interviewed about their drinking, given neuropsychological tests, asked to provide a blood sample, then given a personal profile of results. At six-week follow-up, alcohol consumption was significantly reduced in those who had undergone the check-up compared with a waiting-list control group.

Whilst some clients may respond sufficiently well to advice or feedback, others will undoubtedly require additional skills training: behavioural self-control training, social skills training, relapse prevention, and lifestyle modification. Miller (1989) suggested that it is prudent to try the least intensive intervention first, since this is less intrusive and places fewer demands on resources. If the least intensive intervention fails, then there remains the opportunity to step up to the next level of intensity. The most intensive interventions may be reserved for those who need them.

This suggests that an intervention comprising a series of separate modules might be useful. The outline of a modular programme with components arranged according to Prochaska and DiClemente's (1986) model of stages of change is presented in Figure 3.2. There are several advantages in this type of modular intervention.

1. Matching.
    Clients may enter into the programme at any module and graduate to subsequent modules as appropriate, or exit from the programme at a suitable stage.
2. Motivation.
    The notion of "graduating" from one module to the next may enhance motivation to complete the programme.
3. Repetition.
    Where a client has been slow to assimilate the material presented in any module, the opportunity to repeat that module may be offered.
4. Flexible use of resources.
    Running a complete intervention from start to finish can require a time commitment from the professional which is almost impossible to give. With a modular course, different professionals can be responsible for different modules and the natural breaks which occur between modules can accommodate staff absences for

Figure 3.2 A modular intervention

holidays, training, or other work commitments. In addition, where there is greater demand for one module over any other, this module can be scheduled more frequently.

The subsequent chapters in this book follow the modular programme.

Screening

Three instruments may be used for screening: a simple problem checklist; a psychometric test of alcohol dependence; and a Readiness to Change questionnaire. These are all brief and may be administered to all clients who come into contact with a service in order to identify problems. Where time allows, these questionnaires may be administered in a screening interview, but this will not be possible in all contexts—for example, in some prisons where there is a high population turnover.

Problem Checklist

A problem checklist designed to assess the relationship between drinking and offending, and other problems experienced as a consequence of drinking is presented in Table 3.3. These questions formed the basis of a survey of 100 imprisoned male young offenders, which gives data on the expected percentage of positive responses in a normative sample (McMurran & Hollin, 1989a).

The Short Alcohol Dependent Data (SADD) Questionnaire

A useful adjunct to the problem checklist is the Short Alcohol Dependence Data (SADD) questionnaire, a test designed to measure alcohol dependence (Raistrick, Dunbar & Davidson, 1983; Davidson & Raistrick, 1986). Since it includes questions relating to behavioural and cognitive components of drinking, as well as biological phenomena, the SADD may be particularly useful with populations at the mild—moderate end of the dependence continuum (Davidson, 1987), which is where most young offenders lie. The SADD has been

Table 3.3   Problem checklist

Please answer these questions in relation to your most recent drinking.

	YES	NO	NORMS*
1. Do you think your drinking and offending are related?	...	...	(39%)
2. Please tick any of the following statements which apply to your current offence:			
(a) I had been drinking and I committed an offence that I would not have committed if I had been sober.	...	...	(33%)
(b) The place where I went for a drink was where I got the idea of committing the offence.	...	...	(18%)
(c) Drinking caused problems which made me offend.	...	...	(15%)
(d) I offended so that I could drink.	...	...	(11%)
3. Does drinking cause you any problems other than offending?	...	...	(33%)
If so, what are they?			
(a) Relationship problems	...	...	(17%)
(b) Violence	...	...	(15%)
(c) Financial problems	...	...	(8%)
(d) Health problems	...	...	(6%)
(e) Work problems	...	...	(4%)
(f) Other....................			

*Percentage positive responses in a normative sample of young offenders (McMurran & Hollin, 1989a).

Table 3.4 Short Alcohol Dependence Data (SADD) questionnaire (revised version) (© 1990, Society for the Study of Addiction to Alcohol and Other Drugs, reproduced with permission)

The following questions cover a wide range of topics to do with drinking. Please read each question carefully but do not think too much about its exact meaning. Think about your MOST RECENT drinking habits and answer each question by placing a tick (✓) under the MOST APPROPRIATE heading. If you have any difficulty ASK FOR HELP.

	Never	Sometimes	Often	Nearly always
1. Do you find difficulty getting the thought of drink out of your mind?	...	...	...	...
2. Is getting drunk more important than your next meal?	...	...	...	...
3. Do you plan your day so that you know you'll be able to get a drink?	...	...	...	...
4. Do you start drinking in the morning and drink in the afternoon and evening as well?	...	...	...	...
5. Do you drink for the effect of alcohol without caring what kind of drink you have?	...	...	...	...
6. Do you drink as much as you want without considering what you've got to do next day?	...	...	...	...
7. Given that many problems might be caused by alcohol, do you still drink too much?	...	...	...	...
8. Do you find yourself unable to stop drinking once you start?	...	...	...	...
9. Do you try to control your drinking by giving it up completely for days or weeks at a time?	...	...	...	...
10. The morning after a heavy drinking session do you need your first alcoholic drink to get you going?	...	...	...	...
11. The morning after a heavy drinking session do you wake up with a definite shakiness of your hands?	...	...	...	...
12. After a heavy drinking session do you vomit (throw up)?	...	...	...	...
13. The morning after a heavy drinking session do you go out of your way to avoid people?	...	...	...	...
14. After a heavy drinking session do you see frightening things that you later realise were not real?	...	...	...	...
15. Do you go drinking and next day find you have forgotten what happened the night before?	...	...	...	...

standardised on a male young offender population and, during this process, some revisions have been made to the original wording of the questionnaire to ease comprehension. The revised SADD is presented in Table 3.4.

The SADD correlates well with other measures of alcohol consumption in young offenders, including weekly self-reported alcohol consumption, number of drinking days, and number of days drunk (McMurran, Hollin & Bowen, 1990). This supports the validity of the SADD in measuring alcohol dependence. The SADD has also been shown to be reliable across time, with a test—retest correlation coefficient of 0.88 (McMurran & Hollin, 1989b). This indicates that SADD scores are unlikely to fluctuate unless there is a reason for them to do so, and so the instrument may be useful in evaluating the outcome of interventions.

The SADD comprises 15 items with a four-point frequency scale. Scoring is a simple summation of each item, where Never = 0; Sometimes = 1; Often = 2; and Nearly always = 3. The minimum possible score, therefore, is 0, and the maximum is 45. Raistrick, Dunbar & Davidson (1983) suggest that total scores in the range 0—9 be considered low dependence on alcohol; 10—19 medium dependence; and 20 or greater high dependence. In a sample of 100 male young offenders, the mean SADD score was 8.09 (standard deviation = 7.14: McMurran & Hollin, 1989b). This score may be taken as a bench mark against which to compare any individual young offender's score.

Readiness to Change Questionnaire

The Readiness to Change questionnaire measures the stage of change reached by excessive drinkers (Heather, Gold & Rollnick, 1991). It derives from a longer and more general questionnaire designed to measure stage of change in psychotherapy (McConnaughy et al., 1983; 1989) over which it has the advantages of brevity, so that it is more convenient in screening; and specificity to drinking, so that it is more comprehensible to clients in assessment of alcohol-related problems. (McConnaughy et al.'s questionnaire refers generally to "my problem".)

The 12-item Readiness to Change questionnaire is presented in Table 3.5 and the format for recording scores in Table 3.6. Only three stages are measured by this questionnaire—pre-contemplation, contemplation, and action. Items designed to measure maintenance were eliminated during the development of the questionnaire since they actually prevented the emergence of factors corresponding to the stages of change (Rollnick, Heather, Gold & Hall, 1992).

Table 3.5 Readiness to Change questionnaire (Heather *et al.*, 1991; Rollnick *et al.*, 1992, reproduced by kind permission of the authors)

The following questionnaire is designed to identify how you *personally* feel about your drinking right now. Please read each of the questions below carefully, and then decide whether you agree or disagree with the statements. Please tick the answer of your choice to each question.

	Strongly disagree	Disagree	Unsure	Agree	Strongly agree	For official use only
1. I don't think I drink too much.	☐	☐	☐	☐	☐	☐ P
2. I am trying to drink less than I used to.	☐	☐	☐	☐	☐	☐ A
3. I enjoy my drinking, but sometimes I drink too much.	☐	☐	☐	☐	☐	☐ C
4. Sometimes I think I should cut down on my drinking.	☐	☐	☐	☐	☐	☐ C
5. It's a waste of time thinking about my drinking.	☐	☐	☐	☐	☐	☐ P
6. I have just recently changed my drinking habits.	☐	☐	☐	☐	☐	☐ A
7. Anyone can talk about wanting to do something about drinking, but I am actually doing something about it.	☐	☐	☐	☐	☐	☐ A
8. I am at the stage where I should think about drinking less alcohol.	☐ ☐	☐ ☐	☐ ☐	☐ ☐	☐ ☐	☐ ☐ C
9. My drinking is a problem sometimes.	☐ ☐	☐ ☐	☐ ☐	☐ ☐	☐ ☐	☐ ☐ C
10. There is no need for me to think about changing my drinking.	☐	☐	☐	☐	☐	☐ P
11. I am actually changing my drinking habits right now.	☐	☐	☐	☐	☐	☐ A
12. Drinking less alcohol would be pointless for me.	☐	☐	☐	☐	☐	☐ P

Table 3.6   Readiness to Change questionnaire:
record of scores

Scale scores
Pre-contemplation score   ☐
Contemplation score   ☐
Action score   ☐

Stage of change designation (P, C, or A)   ☐

Readiness to change
Pre-contemplation   ☐   (reverse score)
Contemplation   ☐   (same score)
Action   ☐   (same score)

The Readiness to Change questionnaire is scored by the following
procedure:

Step 1   All items on the questionnaire are scored on a 5-point rating
            scale, as follows:

            RATING   SCORE
            Strongly disagree   −2
            Disagree   −1
            Unsure   0
            Agree   +1
            Strongly agree   +2

Step 2   Items divide into three separate stages, as follows:

            Precontemplation items   1, 5, 10, 12
            Contemplation items   3, 4, 8, 9
            Action items   2, 6, 7, 11

            The score on each scale is calculated by simple summation,
            giving a range of possible scores on each scale from −8
            through zero to +8. If a score is missing for any one item on
            a scale, then the sum of the three items should be multiplied
            by 1.33 to give a pro-rated scale score. If two or more items
            are missing, then the scale score cannot be calculated and
            the stage of change designation will be invalid.

Step 3:   The higher (more positive) the score on any scale, the greater
            the client's agreement with items on that scale. The highest
            score, therefore, gives the *stage of change* designation. In
            the event of a tie, the stage of change is designated to the
            stage further along the continuum of change; that is,

contemplation is preferred over pre-contemplation, and action is preferred over contemplation.

Step 4: The authors point out that increasing scores on the pre-contemplation scale represent a *decreasing* readiness to change, whereas increasing scores on the other two scales represent an *increasing* readiness to change. The stage of change scores can be converted into a *readiness to change* profile simply by reversing the direction (plus or minus) of the pre-contemplation score. (For example, −4 becomes +4; +2 becomes −2.) This allows for direct comparison with scores on the other two scales and shows clearly the relationship between adjacent scales and the relative direction of change across time.

The Readiness to Change questionnaire has been shown to have satisfactory reliability and validity, the latter measured against subjects' own estimations of their stage of change (Rollnick, Heather, Gold & Hall, 1992). Whilst there is good evidence for the validity of the questionnaire and the stages of change model on which it is based, it must be stated that the Readiness to Change questionnaire is still at an early stage of development and there is as yet no evidence for its predictive validity, that is whether it can differentially predict clients' responses to different types of intervention. (McConnaughy *et al.*'s stages of change questionnaire is somewhat better developed in psychometric terms.) Readers who use the Readiness to Change questionnaire could contribute to its development by evaluating its usefulness in assigning clients to specific interventions and measuring change over time.

These three screening questionnaires form the basis for selection for intervention, as portrayed in Figure 3.3. Those who show no evidence of alcohol-related problems *and* score less than 10 on the SADD can be identified as requiring no intervention. Of course, no screening procedure is completely accurate and some people who could benefit from intervention may be missed because they fail to admit any problems. The risk of this may be minimised by conducting screening as part of an interview, but, as already mentioned, this will not always be practically possible.

Those who show evidence of alcohol-related problems on the problem checklist and/or score 10 or more on the SADD may be selected for a brief interview. This interview should focus on presenting feedback from the screening questionnaires, discussing intentions regarding future drinking, and describing the interventions available. Some will accept the offer of further involvement in the programme,

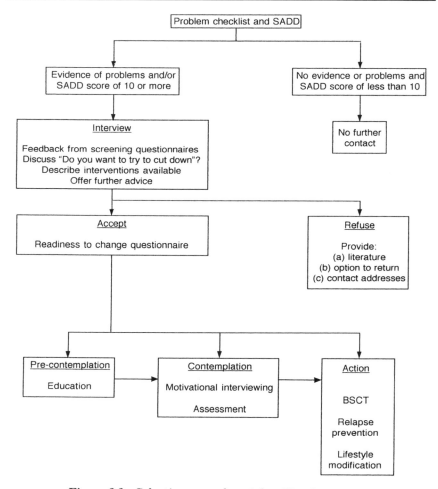

Figure 3.3   Selection procedure (after Heather, 1989)

in which case the Readiness to Change questionnaire may be administered and the offender allocated to the appropriate module. Those who do not wish to participate in the programme may be given advice leaflets and the option to take up the offer of the programme after reading this literature. Contact addresses for other help-giving agencies may also be supplied for future use. Advice literature is available from the Health Education Authority, Alcohol Concern, Councils on Alcohol, and the Advisory Council on Alcohol and Drug Education (TACADE), and a directory of alcohol services is published by Alcohol

Concern. Relevant addresses are given in the List of Resources section.

Summary

The principles of matching are that some people fare better in one type of intervention than others and that if clients are appropriately matched to interventions they are likely to show better outcome than those who are simply given whatever is on offer. Prochaska and DiClemente's (1986) model of stages of change is of practical value in indicating the type of intervention appropriate for an individual in any of these stages.

A modular course may be designed to follow the stages of change, as follows:

1. Education;
2. Motivational interviewing;
3. Assessment;
4. Behavioural self-control training;
5. Social skills training;
6. Relapse prevention;
7. Lifestyle modification.

Clients may enter into the modular programme at any stage, repeat a module, graduate to the next module, or exit from the programme, as appropriate.

Chapter 4

Alcohol Education

Alcohol education is, perhaps surprisingly, a considerably more complex issue than one might expect. Why is this so? When there is pressure to "do something" with offenders who experience alcohol-related problems, education about alcohol and its effects seems a natural first choice. Indeed, a survey of interventions conducted in British prisons reveals this to be true, with a high proportion of both group work and individual interventions, conducted by staff of all professional backgrounds, aimed at educating offenders about alcohol and its effects (McMurran & Baldwin, 1989). The problem is that, despite the prevalent view that alcohol education is a worthwhile pursuit, there are a number of research studies which have led to the conclusion that alcohol education with children and adolescents does not work.

This issue clearly must be addressed before any alcohol education strategy for young offenders can be considered. The aim of this chapter is first to examine the effectiveness of alcohol education; then to define how education might best be applied; and finally to present an alcohol education strategy for use with young offenders.

HOW EFFECTIVE IS ALCOHOL EDUCATION?

In 1974, Stuart investigated the effects of drug education (where alcohol was included as a class of drug) on junior high school pupils. The programme took place one day per week over a 10-week period, and included information about the pharmacology of drugs as well as their physiological effects. Stuart randomly assigned 935 pupils to either the education group or a no-education control group. In comparison with the control group, the education group showed a significantly greater increase in knowledge about drugs and alcohol at the end of the intervention, but also significantly *greater* levels of self-reported drug and alcohol use.

A review of drug and alcohol education programmes by Kinder, Pape and Walfish (1980) showed that this was not an isolated finding.

Where students were concerned, drug and alcohol education pro-grammes undeniably increased levels of knowledge, but also tended to exacerbate rather than reduce drug and alcohol use. Nevertheless, alcohol education with young people continued. Dielman, Shope, Butchart and Campanelli (1986) evaluated an alcohol education programme with 5635 junior high school pupils randomly assigned to either education or a no-education control group. Their course comprised four sessions of 45 minutes duration, and presented information about alcohol and its effects, along with assertiveness training for resisting peer pressure to drink. Again, at the end of the course, the education group showed a significantly greater increase in knowledge about alcohol, yet no differences were apparent in self-reported alcohol use. The authors complimented themselves on the fact that at least alcohol consumption had not been increased through education, and optimistically suggested that the positive effects of education on the young people's alcohol consumption would "appear later" (p. 279).

Hopkins, Mauss, Kearney, and Weissheit (1988) conducted a com-prehensive evaluation of a large-scale alcohol education programme implemented in American junior and senior high schools. The pro-gramme, which lasted three school weeks overall, was designed to (1) increase students' knowledge about alcohol and its effects; (2) encourage attitudes favouring abstinence or moderation; (3) enhance self-esteem; and (4) teach skills for responsible decision-making regarding use of alcohol. Data were collected over three years, using questionnaires, from 6808 students, 3820 of whom had undertaken the programme, and 2988 of whom had not. In the short-term, expo-sure to the alcohol education programme appeared to have a positive effect on measures of knowledge, self-esteem, tolerance of abstinence and moderation, and problem solving, but intentions regarding drinking remained unchanged. Evaluation of the programme in the longer-term showed that only increased levels of knowledge were maintained, and there was no impact on problem behaviour. That is, whilst there was some immediate impact of the education programme on variables thought to be important in mediating alcohol consump-tion, there was little evidence of long-term change, and no impact at all on subsequent drinking behaviour. The authors concluded that the educational programme simply "did not work" (p. 48).

Educational programmes with offenders have typically used only measures of knowledge to evaluate effectiveness. For example, Papandreou, Brooksbank and McLaughlin (1985) described a course run by probation officers for offenders on probation or community service orders. The course—five $1\frac{1}{2}$ hour sessions—aimed to increase participants' knowledge about alcohol and its effects, particularly offending. Those who completed the programme ($n = 229$) showed an overall increase in knowledge about alcohol and its effects, but, of course, a consequent reduction in alcohol consumption cannot be assumed.

USING EDUCATION EFFECTIVELY

It appears, then, that alcohol education is at best ineffective but may even be counterproductive in that it increases rather than decreases alcohol consumption. What might be the possible reasons for this? Firstly, alcohol education programmes may miss those for whom they are intended and, conversely, may include non-problem drinkers. This latter group may be affected by "labelling": that is, if they are included in an alcohol education programme they may assume they are seen to be at-risk for problem drinking, which may then become a self-fulfilling prophecy. Alternatively, education may give rise to a curiosity factor, where young people test out the truth of what they have been told by drinking when they had not previously intended to do so.

Secondly, the message of alcohol education programmes may be too complex to transmit, or inappropriate for the young people at whom such programmes are aimed. Smith (1981) pointed out that the Royal College of Psychiatrists recommends that health educators should attempt to convey that alcohol is a drug; the meaning and implications of dependence on this drug; the nature and extent of harm to both self and others that can be caused by excessive drinking; and the causes of harmful drinking. As Smith has commented, this is quite a formidable task given the interests of the public vis à vis the power of health educators.

Thirdly, alcohol education may be futile without the provision of accompanying information and skills training about *how* to moderate alcohol consumption. Many alcohol education programmes are based on a rational model where the major theoretical conception is that factual information will change a person's beliefs and attitudes and thereby effect behaviour change. However, in a meta-analysis of alcohol education programmes, Rundall and Bruvold (1988) noted that it was mostly the traditional awareness programmes that led to undesired outcomes. The more successful programmes attempted to modify the antecedents to and consequences of alcohol use. It seems, therefore, that it is not helpful to tell young people to "just say no" and expect them to comply.

These problems with alcohol education suggest that a more effective strategy would be (1) to target a specific audience; (2) to present an appropriate message; and (3) to provide a back-up skills training programme.

Targeting a Specific Audience

The question of which offenders to target in educational approaches is answered by the stages of change model described in the previous chapter. That is, it is those who are unaware of or unconcerned by the problems that their drinking may be causing to themselves or others—the pre-contemplators—who may benefit from education. Those in more advanced stages of change, particularly those in the action stage, may actually be put off the idea of engaging in an intervention if, when they expect to receive skills for action, they receive instead only information. It is interesting to note one alcohol education programme for offenders which did result in positive outcomes. Singer (1990) described an alcohol education course for young offenders who were subject to probation orders, in most cases with a special condition of attendance at the educational programme. That is, these offenders were at least recognised as having alcohol-related problems, in comparison to the blanket approach employed in the school studies described above. The six-session course aimed to increase alcohol knowledge, instil responsible attitudes to drinking, and promote safe levels of drinking. At a three-month follow-up assessment, offenders were shown to have increased their knowledge about alcohol and its effects, have more responsible attitudes to drinking, and to have reduced their alcohol consumption. This provides some evidence that appropriate targeting enhances positive outcome.

Conveying an Appropriate Message

There are two important points regarding the message of alcohol education: what the message is, and how the message is conveyed. The message conveyed in education should be relevant to the audience at which it is directed. Where young offenders are concerned, most will not have experienced serious health-related problems, and so emphasis on the physical consequences of chronic heavy drinking may not have much impact. Many young people will also be aware that most drinkers of their acquaintance suffer no alcohol-related health problems. To emphasise the risks of liver cirrhosis, brain damage, and cancers may simply convey the message that it is only a small group of "alcoholics" who need concern themselves about their alcohol consumption and the majority of drinkers (themselves included) have no cause for worry. Whilst it may be appropriate to acknowledge the physical consequences of excessive drinking, greater emphasis should be placed on issues relating to adverse social consequences, including crime.

Some useful information about how to convey the message comes from studies of "psychological reactance" to alcohol education with college students by Bensley and Wu (1991). Reactance is defined as the behavioural response to a situation involving a perceived threat to freedom: any reduction or threat of reduction in a set of free behaviours arouses reactance, which is directed toward re-establishing freedom.

In Bensley and Wu's first study, 535 students (mean age 19.7 years) were categorised as abstainers, occasional drinkers, light/ moderate drinkers, or heavy drinkers. All students received alcohol education in the form of a brief paper which they had to read. This material concluded with either a "high-threat" message or a "low-threat" message. The high-threat message was dogmatic and contained phrases such as "conclusive evidence", "make it obvious", and "any reasonable person must acknowledge the conclusions". The low-threat message was neutral and contained phrases such as "good evidence", "you may wish", and "we believe that these conclusions are reasonable".

Half of the students within each drinking category were given the high-threat message, and half were given the low-threat message. Each condition was again sub-divided, with half being advised to abstain from alcohol and half being advised to control their drinking. After reading the alcohol education material, students were then asked to indicate their future drinking intentions. Results showed that high-threat messages resulted in more drinking intentions than low-threat messages, and that the negative effect was more pronounced where abstinence was recommended. Overall, heavier drinkers showed a greater reactance effect.

In a second study, Bensley and Wu (1991) examined the effects of the type of message on actual drinking, as opposed to intentions regarding drinking. Seventy-four college students (mean age 23.2 years) were categorised as light/moderate or heavy drinkers. These students were then asked to undertake a "memory test", which was in fact a guise for alcohol education. Again, they received either the high-threat or the low-threat message. The same students then went on to do a "taste test", where they were supplied with a variety of beers and asked to rate their preferences. They were allowed to consume as much as they wished in order to form their opinions and their alcohol consumption was surreptitiously monitored. Results showed that, after receiving the high-threat message, male heavy drinkers drank significantly more than male light/moderate drinkers or female subjects.

The studies described above indicate that a dogmatic approach to alcohol education, particularly when combined with an abstinence recommendation, can be counter-productive, particularly for male heavy drinkers. The message conveyed in alcohol education should, therefore, be presented in a non-threatening manner, giving guidelines for sensible drinking rather than an exhortation to abstain altogether.

It is important also to remember the message given in Chapter 3 regarding *how* to teach offenders. Adolescent drinkers are not academically inclined, and school truancy is typical in the personal history of offenders. A disinclination on the part of offenders to undergo formal teaching is, therefore, predictable, and so the use of active teaching methods is indicated. The message regarding sensible drinking will have more impact if it is personal, rather than general, therefore education programmes should include exercises whereby the client examines his or her own drinking patterns. Conveying the message appropriately is as important as conveying the appropriate message.

The Provision of Back-up Skills Training

The interventions described in the following chapters may be considered to comprise the requisite "back-up skills training". In any education course, it is important to give information about additional interventions available.

ALCOHOL EDUCATION GUIDELINES

Introducing the Session

In introducing the session, it is important to state that the aim is to identify sensible drinking guidelines which will minimise adverse effects. This conveys clearly that the message is not one of total abstinence from alcohol, thus avoiding reactance effects, and that suggestions for positive change will be made. As Tether and Robinson (1986) have pointed out, many educational packages are entirely negative— clear about what not to do, but less clear about what to do. Throughout the session, after each exercise or discussion, clients

Table 4.1   Good and bad effects of drinking

Good	Bad
Gives confidence	Get into arguments and fights
Helps cope with problems	Expensive
Sociable	Have accidents
Gets you out of the house	Makes you depressed
Avoids boredom	Makes you promiscuous
Relaxes you	Suffer hangovers
	Miss work next day
	Damages health
	Commit crime

should be instructed to list personal sensible drinking guidelines indicated by the information they have gained.

Effects of Drinking

Drinking alcohol has a variety of effects—physical, psychological, and social—which can be both positive and negative. In promoting a decision to change, possible outcomes should be listed in the form of a chart, as shown in Table 4.1. The list of outcomes may be reviewed in relation to moderate versus heavy drinking: many of the bad effects can be avoided, yet many of the good effects attained, at moderate levels of consumption (see also Chapter 5).

Analysing Alcohol-related Offences

Crime is one obvious negative effect of drinking which demands further analysis. Offenders should be asked to undertake a situational analysis for one or more of their own alcohol-related offences. McGuire and Priestley (1985) recommend a technique called 5-WH: that is, identifying a specific offence and asking the questions Who? What? When? Where? Why? and How? A response sheet is illustrated in Figure 4.1.

The five "W" questions can access information such as who the drinking companions were; what was being drunk; when and where the drinking and offending occurred; and why it happened. The "How?" question can then be aimed at change: "How could offending be avoided in future?" That is, the offender will be encouraged to list personal sensible drinking guidelines.

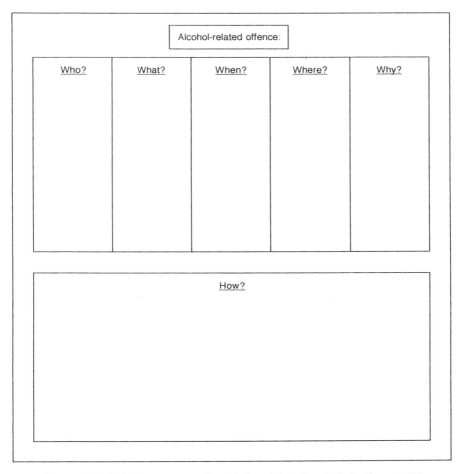

Figure 4.1   5-WH response sheet (after McGuire & Priestley, 1985)

Moderate Drinking

Both of the preceding exercises will convey that moderate drinking is a sensible goal, but "moderation" is a vague term. This can be clarified by calculating alcohol consumption in units. A "standard" drink, that is the measure served in pubs, contains one unit or 8 grammes of pure alcohol. One half pint of beer or lager, one shot of spirits, and one glass of wine each contain one unit of alcohol. (See Chapter 6 for more detailed information about units.) Clients should be asked to calculate their alcohol consumption in units for their most recent week's drinking. Figure 4.2 provides a chart for this purpose.

	Mon	Tue	Wed	Thu	Fri	Sat	Sun
Beer/Lager							
Spirits							
Wine							
Daily total in units							
				Weekly total in units _____			

Figure 4.2   Weekly consumption chart

The safe limits for drinking, as recommended by doctors, are no more than 21 units of alcohol per week for men, and no more than 14 units of alcohol per week for women. Doctors also recommend two or three non-drinking days each week to minimise harm. Alcohol consumed by a pregnant woman can damage the baby and so pregnant women are advised to drink very little, if any, alcohol.

An alcohol fact sheet can be used here to explain and discuss some of the reasons doctors have for recommending these limits. A fact sheet is presented in Table 4.2.

Self-monitoring

Using the chart illustrated in Figure 4.2, offenders should be instructed to monitor their drinking day by day over a period of four to six weeks. Self-monitoring with no additional intervention has proved a therapeutic technique in its own right, possibly through drawing attention to behaviour and triggering a self-regulatory process (Kanfer & Gaelick, 1986).

Drinking and Driving

Having introduced the concept of units of alcohol, it is timely to provide information about drinking and driving. In the UK, the legal upper limit for driving is a blood alcohol concentration (BAC) of 80 milligrammes of alcohol per 100 millilitres of blood. After drinking one standard unit of alcohol, BAC will be between 15 and 20 milligrammes of alcohol per 100 millilitres of blood, depending on weight, body fat, and rate of consumption. Even at BACs under the legal limit, the risk of a traffic accident is considerably elevated for young people (Home Office, 1987), therefore it is difficult to provide guidelines for "safe" levels of drinking when driving, except to say that it is safest to drink no alcohol at all. Offenders should, therefore, be asked to list ways by which they can avoid drinking and driving.

Table 4.2 Alcohol Fact Sheet

Alcohol is a depressant drug. This refers to its effects on the body rather than its psychological effects. Alcohol acts on the brain and nervous system to slow their functioning, which in turn slows down physical reactions. At extreme levels, alcohol can slow physical functioning to the extent that death occurs: the breathing response is suppressed. Therefore, it is unwise to drink large amounts of alcohol quickly. This is usually only possible when drinking spirits. Many drugs—prescribed drugs as well as illicit drugs—exaggerate the effects of alcohol and mixing the two can be dangerous.

What happens to alcohol in the body? Alcohol is quickly absorbed into the blood stream and carried to all parts of the body. Food in the stomach will slow down absorption, but the alcohol will still be absorbed. The blood alcohol concentration after drinking one unit of alcohol is approximately 15–20 milligrammes of alcohol per 100 millilitres of blood. This will vary with weight and how fat a person is: a light person will have a higher blood alcohol concentration than a heavy person after consuming the same amount of alcohol; and a fat person will have a higher blood alcohol concentration than a thin, muscular person after drinking the same amount. Women, who are usually lighter than men and have a higher proportion of fat in their physical make-up, will reach a higher blood alcohol concentration than men after drinking the same amount of alcohol. Alcohol is broken down by the liver at the rate of one unit per hour. This rate is fairly constant and is not affected to any great degree by black coffee or fresh air.

Tolerance to alcohol. If a person drinks regularly, there will be a gradual lessening of the noticeable effects of alcohol. This is called an increased tolerance to alcohol: more alcohol has to be consumed to experience a "buzz". Irrespective of tolerance, alcohol is still entering the bloodstream and blood alcohol levels are no different to those of less tolerant people (of the same weight and body fat) who drink the same amounts. Tolerance is *not* a protection against physical harm: in fact, increased tolerance may place a person at risk of drinking to harmful levels.

Physical effects of alcohol. Alcohol can have a number of adverse physical effects: accidental injury, hangovers, stomach problems, liver damage, and cognitive impairment. Some of these problems are reversible, but if heavy drinking persists then the damage may become permanent.

Table 4.3 Sensible drinking guidelines

1. Keep within 21 units of alcohol per week (men) or 14 units of alcohol per week (women).
2. Do not drink every day.
3. Avoid drinking with friends who frequently get into trouble with the police.
4. Leave pubs and clubs shortly before closing time, especially at weekends.
5. Never drink large amounts of spirits quickly.
6. Do not drive to the pub—you will only be tempted to drive home, and you may be over the limit.
7. Set aside money for living expenses before you go out drinking.
8. Avoid drinking in known trouble-spots.
9. Arrange for a pick-up to take you home—ask a relative or order a taxi.
10. Do not drink when taking drugs.

Sensible Drinking Guidelines

The overall aim of education is to identify sensible drinking guidelines. These should be specified by collating the notes that clients have made throughout the session, adding additional items as necessary. A list of sensible drinking guidelines is presented in Table 4.3.

This list may be used as a method of evaluating the effectiveness of education. Clients may be asked to specify sensible drinking guidelines before education to give a baseline against which to compare the guidelines specified after education. Change may be measured using two criteria: (1) the number of sensible drinking guidelines generated; and (2) the specificity of guidelines generated (for example, "have three alcohol-free days each week" would be a better quality guideline than "drink less").

Skills Training

As mentioned earlier, it is important to follow education with back-up skills training and this is the point at which such an offer could be made. The invitation to join your programme may be accompanied by other options available to the offender (see List of Resources section for a useful directory of alcohol services published by Alcohol Concern).

Summary

Alcohol education approaches can be useful in moving pre-contemplators into the contemplation stage of change. Important points to remember are:

1. To target education at those for whom it is appropriate, that is pre-contemplators and not those who do not experience problems or those who are already in the contemplation or action stage of change;
2. To convey an appropriate message and convey the message appropriately, particularly by using active teaching methods;
3. To offer back-up skills training and not rely on education alone to effect behaviour change.

Chapter 5

Motivational Interviewing

In working with young offenders, one major practical issue is that of motivating clients to reduce their alcohol consumption. The kinds of problems that may be experienced include working with offenders who have been compulsorily and perhaps reluctantly assigned to programmes; dealing with people who may agree to enter programmes primarily to avoid a custodial sentence or to influence reports which might lead to privileges or early parole; and coping with those who appear to deny drink-related problems or who seem to make only half-hearted attempts to change. Although some of these problems may be particular to offenders, the issue of motivating clients to change is recognised as a major problem throughout the alcohol intervention field and, as such, has received a great deal of attention from both practitioners and academics.

In addressing motivation to change, ethical questions inevitably arise. It is often the case that professionals must accept offenders into alcohol programmes even where the offender is not a willing participant or where the professional strongly suspects that the client's agreement with the programme's goals is not genuine. Although many offenders may be difficult to work with because of the uncertainty regarding the reasons for their entry into programmes, their inclusion may be warranted even if they are not volunteers, since the risks to society should they continue to drink and offend are such that personal preference may come second to society's need to control the deviant behaviour. This is not to say that offenders should be forced into intervention programmes and made to comply, but rather that the professional should, using his or her skills, attempt to motivate clients to change.

In this chapter, outcome studies of voluntary versus compulsory interventions will be presented to give some indication of whether it is worth working with compulsorily assigned offenders. Then some of the general problems surrounding motivating clients to change will be addressed. Many of these problems derive from the way professionals construe motivation and so the concept of motivation will be examined, leading to a definition which will be of practical value in determining an approach which can encourage clients to change their drinking behaviour. Finally, specific strategies for increasing motivation will be described.

VOLUNTARY VERSUS COMPULSORY INTERVENTION

In working with offenders, some clients do not enter programmes voluntarily, but because the courts have ordered them to do so or because of pressure from family, friends or legal advisors. Some professionals are reluctant to accept clients who have been compulsorily ordered into interventions, believing that the motivation of the coerced client is less than that of volunteers and so the outcome will necessarily be less successful. Such a conclusion may, however, be unwarranted. There is evidence to suggest that drinking problems can be successfully dealt with in people who have entered programmes without complete freedom of choice.

Miller (1978), in evaluating the effectiveness of three types of controlled drinking intervention, used both self-referred and court-referred clients in his study. The latter were referred to the alcohol programme as an alternative to sentencing for driving whilst intoxicated. Both the court-referred clients and the self-referrals subsequently reduced their drinking and maintained the change at one year follow-up. Watson *et al.* (1988) studied male "alcoholics" who had completed an abstinence-oriented in-patient programme. In comparing those who had made self-referrals with those who had been referred by court order or who had referred themselves under pressure from family, friends, or others, no significant differences were found in control over drinking in an 18-month follow-up period. Indeed, the coerced group tended, if anything, to show slightly better outcome. Vogler, Compton and Weissbach (1976) compared referrals from legal sources (courts, probation officers, attornies) with referrals from mental health professionals and self-referrals in a programme aimed at teaching participants how to drink less. Of these, 72% of legal referrals and 70% of non-legal referrals completed the programme. Even though those referred through legal channels reported a significantly smaller pre-intervention alcohol consumption than non-legal referrals, the amount of reduction in alcohol intake was similar for both groups of clients, with the legal clients drinking significantly less at follow-up one year after the programme. Hoffman, Ninonuevo, Mozey and Luxenberg (1987) compared the performance of court-referred driving-whilst-intoxicated offenders with non-offender outpatients in a programme aimed at total abstinence from alcohol. Court-referred clients were more likely to complete the programme and at six-month follow-up reports of abstinence were 78% for the court-referred group and 81% for the non court-referred group.

These studies suggest that a court order for treatment may increase the likelihood of clients completing an alcohol intervention programme, and a successful outcome seems as likely with court-ordered clients as with referrals from other sources. Therefore, these results challenge the belief that success in alcohol interventions depends on the person entering with a desire to change: positive results can be achieved with clients who are compulsorily referred to an intervention programme. It may be that forcing a person to enter a programme addressing drinking and related problems is in itself a motivational technique, but, whatever the source of the referral, once a person has been accepted into an intervention the challenge is to encourage that person to make changes to his or her drinking behaviour.

THE TRAIT MODEL OF MOTIVATION

It is important first of all to examine carefully what is meant by the term "motivation". Miller (1985) suggests that motivation is a term traditionally used to describe the client's willingness to enter into a programme and comply with its demands, and success in achieving the programme's goals. "Lack of motivation" describes the opposite: failure to admit any problem (denial), reluctance to receive help, failure to comply with an intervention programme, and resistance to behaviour change. As Miller (1983b) points out, this may be a comfortable way for the professional to view motivation: successes are attributed to the skills of the counsellor or the quality of the programme so long as the client is motivated to change, while failures are attributed to the deficiencies of the client, who fails because of lack of motivation.

Such a construction of motivation is a trait model: that is, motivation is seen as a characteristic that resides within the client. This model presents several serious drawbacks to successful outcome for some clients.

1. *The client is blamed for failure.*
   The client is judged as a failure because of having insufficient motivation. Having been exposed as deficient, the client may then be less likely to attempt change, since overcoming this deficiency is seen as impossible, both by the client and by others.

2. *The client is not credited with success.*
   When a client does succeed in changing his or her behaviour, the credit may be given to the programme or the counsellor, thus minimising the client's belief in his or her own ability to change. Where a client believes that change is due to an external agent and not due to his or her own actions, then that change is less likely to be maintained.

3. *Dismissing a client until help is requested.*
   Potential clients whose motivation is suspected to be lacking may be excluded from programmes. People with alcohol-related problems may not want professional help for a number of reasons: their peers may mock them for seeking help; they may assume that the goals of intervention will be too severe and unacceptable to them; they may assume that the method of intervention is going to be difficult or painful for them; they may fear that the problems they will have to face if they stop or reduce their drinking (for example, boredom or loneliness) will be worse than the problems that result from their drinking; they may believe there is no way possible of changing their drinking and therefore see no point in the intervention. To dismiss clients as unmotivated rules out many whose behaviour might be improved, bringing substantial benefits to the individual, to society, or to both.

4. *Interventions remain under-developed.*
   Selecting only those clients who appear motivated to change leads to interventions that are effective primarily with this group. Indeed, it has been said that if the client is motivated, then successful outcome is highly probable, irrespective of what the professional actually does. This leads to the situation where clients who are bad bets, that is who "lack motivation", if they are accepted onto programmes at all, may receive interventions which do not address issues specifically relevant to them.

THE BEHAVIOURAL MODEL OF MOTIVATION

Motivation to change can be viewed in an entirely more constructive way. It is clear that motivation is not constant but rather it fluctuates over time. For example, it is often said that "alcoholics" must "hit rock bottom" before they can accept the need to change; that is, their situation must become so intolerable as to inspire them with motivation to change. The very notion of circumstances changing such that they are no longer tolerable, thus leading to an increase in motivation to change drinking behaviour, suggests that motivation is not a static

Table 5.1 The motivational balance

Positive effects of drinking	Negative effects of drinking
Relief from boredom	Physical problems
Social facilitation	Financial hardship
Tension reduction	Relationship problems
Relief of physiological discomfort	Trouble with the law
Enjoyment of feeling drunk	Arguments and fights

or a stable trait. Motivation to change can more usefully be construed as the outcome of an interaction among the drinker, the drinking behaviour, and external factors in his or her life.

As illustrated in Table 5.1, motivation to change may be construed in terms of a balance, with the positive effects of drinking weighing on one side and the negative effects of drinking weighing on the other. None of these effects is permanent: there will be changes depending upon an individual's current situation, including the status of inter-personal relationships, employment, accommodation, finance, and arrests and convictions.

If it is true that motivation is not static, then it is useful for professionals to identify what strategies they could use to encourage change and what strategies they should avoid if they are not to discourage change. The aim should be to tip the motivational balance so that the likelihood of drinking is decreased.

Motivation to change may be summarised as follows. Motivation can be defined as *the probability that a person will enter into, continue, and adhere to a specific change strategy* (Miller, 1985). Motivation is the outcome of an interaction that takes in the drinker, the drinking behaviour, and external factors such as relationships, finance, and legal consequences. These factors are not stable across time and, as they change, so motivation will change. It is possible to alter a person's motivation to change by addressing the factors involved in drinking behaviour.

MOTIVATIONAL STYLE

Miller, Sovereign and Krege (1988) described three general processes in creating the conditions for increasing motivation to change: affirmation, awareness, and alternatives. These three motivational processes aim at enhancing self-esteem, creating a discrepancy between the client's present situation and how he or she would like things to be, and enhancing self-efficacy.

Affirmation

This refers to an empathic, optimistic, and helpful stance by the counsellor. An affirmative approach requires the professional to accept the client as a responsible person, capable of making rational decisions about his or her drinking, and capable of making efforts to change. An affirmative style is consistent with enhancing the client's *self-esteem*: that is, the client should feel that he or she is worth changing.

Self-esteem may be defined as the worth an individual bestows on himself or herself and can range from self-acceptance to self-rejection (Hargie, Saunders & Dickson, 1981). The process of self-evaluation from which self-esteem levels are derived is based upon social comparison and social reinforcement. We compare our assets, capabilities, and achievements with those of others, and self-esteem depends partly upon our perceived standing in comparison with other people. Self-esteem also depends upon how others react to us: positive, rewarding relationships lead to high self-esteem, whereas negative, punishing relationships lead to low self-esteem. People with alcohol-related problems have been shown to have low self-esteem (Hull & Schnurr, 1986).

Exposure to a positive interpersonal experience may be expected to raise self-esteem and this may be best achieved in the counselling situation through affirmation. An affirmative style is best described by Rogers (1973) in his client-centred approach to therapy. A counsellor can facilitate constructive change in the client by bringing to the relationship the following ingredients:

Congruence. The counsellor is aware of his or her own feelings in the counselling situation and can relate to the client as a "real person". This requires that the counsellor does not hide behind a front or play a role, but rather should express his or her genuine thoughts and feelings. Even negative thoughts and feelings may be expressed, although sensitivity is important. Rogers (1973) gives the example of a counsellor who is bored with a client. He suggests that the counsellor should determine why he or she feels boredom, for example, because the client is too remote. In expressing the need to gain closer contact with the client, the counsellor exposes a barrier in the counselling relationship and thus opens opportunities for further development. The counseller has related to the client as a "real person", that is real but imperfect, which is both genuine and congruent.

Empathy. The counsellor can communicate an accurate understanding of the client's private world in such a way as to encourage further exploration. The counsellor may voice feelings of which the client is only vaguely aware, for example "you seem to have been hurt by that" or "it sounds as if you are angry about this". Empathic understanding validates the client's experiences and creates opportunities for further disclosure. Empathy should not be confused with sympathy ("you poor thing!") which is patronising, or with identification ("I know exactly how you feel!") which is false; neither of these things is helpful.

Positive regard. The counsellor respects and values the client as a person. The counsellor should demonstrate this positive regard by paying selective attention to the client's assets, capabilities and achievements. This involves accurate but selective reflection of what the client says. It is neither appropriate to gloss over problems ("you've got a lot going for you and I'm sure things will be just fine"), nor to take a pessimistic line ("you've got real problems here and the situation looks bad"). Instead, it is appropriate to acknowledge problems frankly along with emphasising the client's assets. An example might be: "drinking and getting into fights is a problem and <u>you recognise that it is. You have a supportive family</u> and <u>you'd like to try to make some changes in your life.</u>" The positive regard statements are underlined.

Although it is required that the counsellor should value the person, this does not mean that the counsellor must approve of everything the client does. Indeed, it is important to distinguish between the person and the behaviour to avoid labelling. Where the person and the behaviour are equated, a judgment such as "you are bad" may follow, whereas separating the person from the behaviour leads to a different perspective, for example, "you are a worthwhile person, but this aspect of your behaviour cannot be condoned". This is particularly important in working with offenders.

When the counsellor communicates congruence, empathy, and positive regard to the client, the conditions are created for the enhancement of self-esteem.

Awareness

This is the process of increasing the drinker's consciousness of personal risk. By providing information, commenting on faulty beliefs, and drawing attention to inconsistencies in the client's explanation of behaviours, the professional can make apparent the *discrepancy* between the desired goal and the client's present state.

Motivation has already been described as a balance of the positive and negative outcomes of drinking (see Table 5.1). Most people are aware of the factors on each side of their own personal balance, but where they continue to drink heavily they may use strategies to emphasise the positive effects and minimise the negative effects. Common strategies are to avoid thinking about the negative effects, to minimise the extent of their disruptive influence on life, and to attribute their cause to something other than drinking. These strategies may be seen as ways of reducing *cognitive dissonance*, that is the discrepancy between the person's actual behaviour and his or her beliefs, values, attitudes, and feelings. Where a person acknowledges the negative effects of his or her behaviour, feelings of discomfort are created. In attempting to reduce these feelings of discomfort, behaviour change rather than minimisation of the negative effects is the desired goal. The counsellor must, therefore, assist the client in acknowledging the negative effects of drinking and, having thus created a discrepancy between what the client is doing now and what the client would like in his or her life, skills must be taught to enable the client to reduce the dissonance by behaviour change.

Alternatives

It is important that the client should see that there are realistic alternatives to his or her current behaviour. By suggesting alternative possibilities, describing the goals and the nature of interventions on offer, and negotiating with the client what might produce the best overall result, the professional is most likely to engage the client in an intervention. Presenting alternatives is consistent with enhancing the client's *self-efficacy*: that is, the client should feel that he or she is capable of making changes.

Self-efficacy may be defined as a person's evaluation of his or her competence to perform a task in a specific situation (Bandura, 1977b). Efficacy judgments influence what people choose to do, how much effort they will put into the task, and how long they will persist in the face of obstacles. When self-efficacy is low, that is when a person believes himself or herself unable to perform a task successfully, then he or she will feel apprehension in difficult situations and either avoid them or make little effort to meet the challenge. Conversely, when self-efficacy is high, a person will feel relaxed and seek out situations in which he or she feels competent and, should difficulties arise, will rise to meet the challenge.

Self-efficacy judgments are based on four main sources of information: (1) one's own past performance; (2) observation of others' performance; (3) instruction; and (4) emotional arousal. That is, to feel competent to perform a task effectively a person must know what to do, have evidence from others' performance that it can be done, feel relaxed enough to do it, and experience personal mastery. Self-efficacy can be increased, therefore, by a gradual process of instruction, modelling, and practice.

The motivational process of presenting alternatives begins to enhance a client's self-efficacy by focusing on goals and tasks which he or she feels competent to achieve. Debilitating pre-conceptions such as the need for abstinence or the abandonment of enjoyable social activities as necessary solutions to drink-related problems are challenged. Thus, the counsellor can influence what the client chooses to do. Subsequent skills training in support of the client's choice will increase the likelihood of successful outcomes: this is of major importance since successful performance of a task has the greatest impact on self-efficacy judgement.

To summarise, a motivational style creates the conditions for behaviour change in that the client is treated as a responsible individual who is worth the effort of changing and is capable of making behavioural changes but may require help to do so. The professional helps the client to become aware of the effects of his or her behaviour and provides information about the possible alternatives from which he or she can choose, including alternative therapeutic goals and interventions.

Before going on to describe specific motivational techniques, it is worth issuing a warning against strategies which should be avoided since they typically serve to reduce rather than enhance client motivation.

STRATEGIES TO AVOID

There are several strategies which are inconsistent with a motivational style and which are important to avoid.

Do not label the client. It is not desirable that the client should be forced to admit to being an "alcoholic" or even a "problem drinker", since the client may not share the professional's "diagnosis" and confrontation may lead to the phenomenon of "denial". Labels such as "alcoholic" or "problem drinker" may impair the client's perceived ability to change since the problems implied by these labels appear to require medical or other professional expertise and to be beyond the client's personal control. Labels may also imply intervention goals and methods to which some clients may feel resistance, for example, abstinence as the recommended goal and long-term intensive therapy.

Do not use a confrontational approach. Most drinkers will be able to list both positive and negative effects of their drinking, even where they express little desire to reduce their alcohol consumption. Where problems are minimised or not readily admitted by the client, confrontation is sometimes used to expose the client to the professional's perception of reality. When the professional adopts such a confrontational approach, the client is forced into defending the opposite position. Given that motivation is a balance of the positive and negative effects of drinking, and the client can usually see both sides of the balance, for the professional to take the side of the negative effects will elicit from the client a defence of the positive effects. One danger of confrontation lies in strengthening the client's beliefs that drinking is not a problem: as the individual argues that his or her drinking has positive effects, so those arguments become more sophisticated and refined and more convincing to the client himself or herself.

Do not use scare tactics. In raising awareness, the use of scare tactics is inadvisable. A scare tactic might be a warning such as "if you continue to drink and get into fights you will find yourself on a murder charge one day", or "the amount you are drinking is going to kill you: your liver will simply pack up eventually". Such scare tactics often serve only to raise anxiety to a level where anxiety reduction rather than change of problem behaviour is the route of escape. Anxiety reduction may be achieved by the avoidance of thinking about drinking as a problem (that is, by reverting to the pre-contemplation stage of change), or may even be achieved by increased alcohol consumption in those for whom drinking is commonly used as a means of anxiety reduction.

Do not force your goals on the client. A client may choose to aim for abstinence or for a reduction in alcohol consumption from previous levels. Whilst abstinence may be viewed by the professional as the best choice in some cases, particularly where there is organic damage or where a client has failed to control drinking in the past, a client may not wish to abstain and, after ensuring that the client is properly informed to make a choice, the professional must respect the client's wishes. Similarly, a client may prefer to aim for abstinence where the professional would recommend controlled drinking based on factors such as low dependence on alcohol and the social nature of drinking, and again the professional must ultimately respect the client's choice. There is some evidence that goal preference is a predictor of success in interventions (Orford & Keddie, 1986). As long as a client chooses to make some positive change, however small, either to the level of alcohol consumption or to the social or situational circumstances of drinking which may lead to criminal behaviour, then accept this goal. Goals may be reviewed regularly, and further change can be encouraged over time.

MOTIVATIONAL INTERVIEWING

The aim of motivational interviewing is to increase the probability that a person will enter into, continue, and adhere to a specific change strategy. The practice of motivational interviewing is thoroughly described in a book by Miller and Rollnick (1991) entitled *Motivational Interviewing: Preparing People to Change Addictive Behavior*. The basic elements of this approach are presented here. Within the overall motivational style of affirmation, raising the clients awareness, and suggesting alternatives, there are specific strategies which may be used to enhance motivation.

Preparation: Removing Barriers

Prior to making appointments for interviews, it is as well to address the practicalities of the situation. For some clients, obstacles may arise to prevent attendance at meetings and it is important, therefore, to address issues such as cost of travelling, negotiating time off work with employers, child care, and accessibility of the meeting place. In institutions, issues such as loss of work opportunities, loss of earnings, and time-table clashes with other activities will need to be addressed.

Eliciting Self-motivational Statements

The confrontational approach, as has already been stated, has drawbacks in that the client will be placed in the position of having to defend his or her behaviour and so confrontation may serve to elicit denial of problems and even to strengthen problem behaviour since the client, when put in a position of arguing *for* drinking, is likely to convince himself or herself of the positive aspects. The skill is to do the opposite: to put the client in the position of stating the *negative*

effects of drinking and the *benefits of change.* In motivational interviewing, it is the client—not the professional—who presents the arguments for change. The principle behind this is captured in the
statement "I learn what I believe as I hear myself talk."

Miller (1983b) recommends that professionals should aim to elicit
self-motivational statements. These are statements generated by the
client which contain one or more of the following features: (1) recognition of a problem; (2) concern about the problem; and (3) intention to
change. Examples of self-motivational statements are:

—"I suppose drink does interfere with some things in my life."
—"I think I'm drinking too much."
—"Things are getting bad".
—"I'm going to have to look at my drinking."
—"I must avoid getting into trouble with the law."
—"I would like to take a couple of drinks and leave it at that."

When the client produces a self-motivational statement, it should be
reinforced by the professional. Nodding your head, saying "Yes" or
"Uh-huh", or offering a supportive statement (eg "It's good that
you're thinking about this"; "That must be difficult") are all
reinforcers.

Strategies for eliciting self-motivational statements are as follows:

Evocative Questions

Assume that the client recognises that there are problems and that
change is desirable. Examples of questions which might derive from
this assumption are:

—"What concerns you about your drinking?"
—"What problems do you associate with your drinking?"
—"What changes would you like to make?"

These questions may be compared with others aimed at eliciting the
same information but phrased without assuming that the client
already recognises that there is a problem and that change is
desirable:

—"Are you concerned about your drinking?"
—"Does your drinking cause you problems?"
—"Do you think you should do something about your drinking?"

By assuming that the client recognises a problem and the need for change this reduces the likelihood of eliciting denial and enhances the likelihood of eliciting self-motivational statements; that is, you are less likely to get negative answers ("no", "nothing", or "none") in response to the first set of questions.

List the Pros and Cons of Drinking

As people move through the stages of change, their perceptions of the balance of the advantages and disadvantages of their behaviour alters (Prochaska & DiClemente, 1986). In promoting a decision to change, elucidation of the pros and cons of drinking will help to highlight the link between the client's present behaviour and the negative outcomes which he or she wishes to avoid. That is, the client will be assisted in acknowledging the discrepancy between present drinking and a preferred absence of negative outcomes. Furthermore, alternatives may be introduced by checking the availability of each of the items on the pros and cons lists at different levels of consumption: abstinence, moderation, and heavy drinking. Usually, most of the positive effects are seen as available at abstinence or moderate drinking levels (for example, meeting people, boredom relief, and relaxation) and at the same time many of the negative effects can be avoided (for example, overspending, crime, and hangovers). This exercise may be done using a simple chart, as illustrated in Table 5.2.

This outcome analysis technique has been used in group alcohol programmes with offenders and was rated the most useful component of the intervention (McMurran & Thomas, 1991). Interestingly, a similar technique has been successfully applied with young offenders in aggression control programmes (McDougall & Boddis, 1991).

Acknowledge the Positive Effects of Drinking for the Client

All too often professionals fail to acknowledge the positive effects of drinking and this can make the client feel that his or her behaviour is abnormal or irrational. The affirmative approach requires acceptance of the client as a rational person and acknowledging good reasons for the problem behaviour serves to do this. The types of statement which derive from this acknowledgement are:

—"Drinking seems to help you socialise."
—"Drinking seems to help you fill your time."
—"Drinking seems to be good fun."

Table 5.2   The pros and cons of drinking

Pros	A	M	H*	Cons	A	M	H*

*Tick whether this outcome likely if:
(A)   abstinent,
(M)   if drink moderately, and
(H)   if drink heavily.

Such statements are likely to elicit a "Yes, but..." response, with the conditional clause being a self-motivational statement. An example is "Yes, drinking does help me socialise, but I get drunk and go too far then I get into fights."

Elaboration

When a self-motivational statement is given, it is useful to ask the client to elaborate upon the theme, which helps to elicit additional self-motivational statements. This can be done by asking for clarification and specific examples as follows:

Example

CLIENT. I get really paranoid when I've had too much to drink.

COUNSELLOR. What do you mean by paranoid?

CLIENT. Well, I take everything too personally.

COUNSELLOR. Can you give me a recent example of that?

Paradoxical Challenge

Used judiciously, paradoxical challenge can elicit self-motivational statements. A paradoxical challenge may be understood as the professional voicing the client's doubts and is appropriate when the client is dismissive of his or her problems. Two examples of paradoxical challenge are:

CLIENT. I get into fights after I've been drinking on a Saturday night, but so do most of my mates.

COUNSELLOR. If everyone does it, perhaps it's not a problem.

and

CLIENT. My parents complain, my girlfriend complains, and my boss complains, but that's their problem.

COUNSELLOR. Perhaps you're right. Perhaps you shouldn't think about changing just for them.

Such challenges place the client in the position of having to expand on the negative effects of drinking and persuading the professional of his or her motivation to change. Responses to the above examples might be: "well, it's a problem for me when I get lifted by the police", and "but I don't want to get chucked out of the house or lose my girlfriend or lose my job".

Paradoxical challenge is *not* appropriate when the client expresses low self-efficacy in statements such as "I don't think I can change." A paradoxical challenge such as "well, maybe you can't", in this case, would serve only to reduce the client's self-efficacy still further, which is not the aim of motivational interviewing.

Role-reversal

Motivational statements of a slightly different sort can be elicited by changing roles. The client acts in the role of counsellor and persuades the counsellor, who is acting as client, to look at his or her problem. Here, the counsellor-acting-client presents the real client's arguments for him or her to challenge.

Creating Dissonance

The disparity between the client's current situation and how he or she would like things to be can be elucidated by looking back and looking forward. Looking back to times before the problem emerged can be encouraged by asking questions such as "what were things like before you started drinking heavily? Did you get into fights in those days?" Looking forward is to ask people what changes they would like to see in future using questions such as "how would you like your life to be a year from now?"

Summarising

At intervals, it is useful to summarise the information gathered. Present the summary as a means of checking that information has been gathered accurately by saying "let me just check that I've got everything straight so far", or simply as a review, "let me summarise where we've got to so far". One aim of summarising is to emphasise and thereby reinforce self-motivational statements. Summaries should, therefore, be selective repetitions of the client's self-motivational statements. A second aim is to restructure the content of the interview to encourage the client to continue investigating the possibility of change. For example, a client may express self-defeating statements such as "I've tried cutting down my drinking before and it's just hopeless". This statement could be restructured to enhance the client's feelings of self-efficacy, for example "you seem motivated to cut down your drinking judging by previous attempts, but perhaps you have yet to discover exactly how you can achieve success".

Moving Forward

Up to this point the intervention described has been non-directive but this has its limitations: the need for more direction in the process soon becomes apparent. Throughout the motivational interview, well-timed feedback, presentation of goal and intervention options, and advice, can be helpful in moving the client from the contemplation stage into making a decision to change.

Assessment

Although assessment is typically viewed as the initial stage in the process of selection for and design of an intervention, the interaction between the client and the professional, along with the contribution to raising awareness of the personal risks of drinking, can enhance the individual's motivation for and commitment to change (Donovan, 1988). Assessment procedures are described more fully in Chapter 6 where it will become clear that information collected from self-report, questionnaires, and self-monitoring will eventually be used in a functional analysis of the problem behaviour. In the meantime, information from these assessment procedures may be presented to the client to raise awareness of the personal risks involved in drinking.

The style of presenting information is important. Rather than confront the client with the negative effects of drinking, a less adversarial strategy is to present the facts objectively so that the client may assess their meaning for himself or herself. Examples of the types of statement that might derive from this approach are:

— "Doctors say that three or four pints of beer three or four times a week is about the safe limit for men's drinking. Your drinking diary shows that you drink more than the recommended limit."
— "Looking at all the offences you have been telling me about, it seems that most occur on weekend nights after you have been drinking."
— "The average score on the Short Alcohol Dependence Data questionnaire is 8. Your score is 15."

Such statements allow the client to consider the personal implications of the information you are presenting without feeling defensive. Remember, it is important that the client should not be placed in the position of defending his or her drinking since defensive statements are arguments *for* drinking, unlike self-motivational statements which are arguments *against* drinking.

Alternatives

Decisions to change will be influenced by the client's awareness of possible goals—abstinence, moderation, or just changes in drinking patterns—and methods of working towards these goals—self-help, support groups, or alcohol intervention programmes. Clients benefit more when they choose for themselves from a range of options.

Advice

Simple advice may be sufficient to effect the desired change in behaviour for some clients. Edwards *et al.* (1977) compared men who were recommended by a psychiatrist to abstain from drinking and told that the responsibility for attainment of this goal lay with them, against men who received intensive therapy. In both conditions the men reduced their drinking, with no significant differences between the advice and intensive intervention groups. Chick, Lloyd and Crombie (1985) identified patients in a general hospital population as having a current alcohol problem. Of those who were given a 30—60 minute counselling session by a trained nurse, fewer showed alcohol-related problems at a one-year follow-up than for those in a no-intervention control group.

The FRAMES Model

Miller and Sovereign (1989) neatly summarise the main elements of motivating clients to change using the acronym "FRAMES".

FEEDBACK: Give personal feedback to the client about his or her drinking and related problems.

RESPONSIBILITY: Emphasise that the client is responsible for change. No one can do this for him or her.

ADVICE: Give non-confrontational advice about drinking and associated risks.

MENU OF ALTERNATIVES: Present the client with a choice of goals and a range of methods for achieving them.

EMPATHY: Raise the client's self-esteem by using a client-centred, affirmative style.

SELF-EFFICACY: Encourage the client to believe that he or she has the power to change.

For some clients, motivational interviewing which includes feedback and advice may be a sufficient intervention. Miller and Sovereign (1989) described a Drinker's Check-Up, comprising two visits to a clinic for assessment and feedback conducted using motivational interviewing techniques. In comparing participants with those on a waiting-list control, alcohol consumption was significantly reduced at a six-week follow-up. In a second study of the Drinker's Check-Up, a motivational interviewing style was compared with feedback conducted in a directive, confrontational fashion, with motivational interviewing proving superior in reducing alcohol consumption.

It can be concluded that whilst some clients may require no more than advice and feedback using motivational interviewing techniques, others will require more intensive intervention programmes and the rest of this book aims to offer help in their design and evaluation.

Summary

Motivation is best understood not as a client trait but rather an interaction among the drinker, the drinking behaviour, and external factors such as relationships, finances, and legal consequences. These factors are not stable over time and, as they change, so motivation will change. It is the professional's role to alter a person's motivation to change by addressing the factors involved in drinking.

Using an affirmative counselling style, the professional should raise the client's awareness of personal risk from drinking and suggest alternatives. Motivational interviewing aims to elicit self-motivational statements from the client through the strategy of placing him or her in the position of describing the negative effects of drinking and thereby suggesting change. Self-motivational statements should finally be consolidated into decision making.

The techniques of eliciting self-motivational statements are:

1. Avoid operating in a confrontational style by assuming that the client recognises that there are problems and that change is desirable.

2. Highlight the discrepancy between present drinking and a preferred absence of negative outcomes by asking the client to list the pros and cons of drinking.

3. Place the client in the position of describing the negative effects of drinking by acknowledging the positive effects on the client's behalf.

4. Follow through self-motivational statements by asking the client to elaborate.

5. Encourage the client to express motivation by using paradoxical challenge where minimisation of problems is evident.

6. Reverse roles: allow the client to role-play the counsellor.

7. Create dissonance by looking back to times before the problem emerged and looking forward to how the client would like life to be.

8. Reinforce self-motivational statements by restructuring self-defeating statements and emphasising positive statements in summaries.

9. Raise the client's awareness of personal risk by providing objective feedback.

10. Encourage decision-making by presenting a range of alternative goals and interventions, and by offering advice.

Chapter 6

Assessment

There are several important purposes in gathering information about a client's drinking and related behaviours, including crime. Assessment is important firstly for efficient identification of problems, that is, as a *screening* method. Where there is an indication that a problem exists, clients may be selected on the basis of the initial screening for a comprehensive assessment. Secondly, the information gathered in assessment may be used in giving *feedback* to the client so that he or she may judge his or her drinking according to norms and recommended limits. Thirdly, information from assessment may be integrated in a *functional analysis* providing a framework for understanding the client's problems. Fourthly, information may be used in *matching* a client with an appropriate intervention. Finally, pre-intervention assessment measures may be compared with post-intervention measures in *evaluation* of the outcome of an intervention. It is important to realise that assessment is not a discrete stage which is completed within the first interview, but rather that assessment and intervention merge with one another. Methods for assessing various aspects of drinking and related behaviours are presented throughout this book and this chapter may be viewed simply as a starting point. Before describing specific assessment procedures for use with young offenders, first it is necessary to consider some important general issues.

AN INTRODUCTION TO ASSESSMENT PROCEDURES

In any assessment, information is required about the precise patterns of the behaviour under study, the social and situational contexts in which the behaviour occurs, and the various consequences of the behaviour. The measures used to collect such information should fit the following four main criteria:

1. Validity: they should measure what it is intended they should measure;

2. Reliability: they should show consistency when data are collected under similar circumstances;
3. Usefulness: the information should be relevant to a purpose;
4. Practicability: their use should be feasible within the practical constraints of the situation.

A variety of assessment techniques is available, each of which may be more or less satisfactory according to these four criteria. No single assessment technique is perfect and it is important to understand the strengths and limitations of each so that appropriate measures may be selected and used to the best effect.

ASSESSMENT METHODS

Direct observation

Direct observation of behaviour is often seen as the methodological ideal; however, in assessment of drinking and related crime there are obstacles to direct observation. Observing drinking *per se* is often impossible, for example, when the offender is detained in an institution where alcohol consumption is not permitted. Even where direct observation is theoretically possible, it is usually not practicable since it would involve considerable intrusion into the offender's life and would require an inordinate amount of the professional's time. In addition to these practical problems, it is unlikely that any offender would behave in his or her normal manner whilst being observed by a "fly on the wall". Where assessment of alcohol-related offending is concerned, there are clearly ethical problems in setting out to observe offending behaviour. Because of these difficulties in direct observation, professionals must, for the most part, rely on indirect sources of information, the most important source being the client himself or herself.

Interviews and diaries

Many assessment procedures rely heavily on clients' self-reports in the form of interviews (retrospective self-report) and diaries (concurrent self-report). Whilst doubts have been raised in the scientific literature about the validity of self-report, there is, in fact, usually no alternative source of information and professionals remain dependent upon clients' accounts of their own behaviour.

The validity of adult prisoners' self-reported alcohol consumption has been studied by comparing self-report data with information gathered from prisoners' relatives. The degree of concordance suggests that prisoners give reasonably valid self-reports. Guze, Tuason, Stewart and Picken (1963) reported 85% overall agreement between prisoners' and relatives' reports of quantity and frequency of drinking. Myers (1983) reported a correlation of 0.68 for prisoners' and wives'/cohabitees' reports of alcohol consumption on the day of the offence.

Young offenders' self-reports of alcohol consumption have been studied by examining the reliability of and consistency among a variety of different measures collected for research purposes. McMurran, Hollin, and Bowen (1990) asked 56 male young offenders to report, based on a "typical week", how many days they had consumed alcohol, how many days they were drunk, and how much alcohol they had consumed. After 96 days, these young offenders were asked the same questions again, and were also asked to complete the Short Alcohol Dependence Data (SADD) questionnaire (which is described more fully in Chapter 3). Quantity—frequency measures of alcohol consumption were reliable over time and different indices of alcohol consumption (drinking days, days drunk, units consumed, and SADD score) correlated significantly with each other. Although test—retest reliability and consistency among different measures do not provide sufficient evidence for validity, they are necessary to it, and so these results allow cautious confidence in the validity of young offenders' self-reported alcohol consumption, at least when collected for research purposes.

Because professionals are dependent on client self-report, it is important to ensure that the conditions under which self-report is collected are those which maximise the likelihood of validity. Until recently, validity studies have been designed to address the question "are self-reports of alcohol consumption valid?" That such a question should be posed at all betrays the generalisations applied to client groups, for example, that "alcoholics" minimise their alcohol consumption and deny their problems, or that offenders over-estimate their alcohol consumption to use drinking as an excuse for their offending.

What has recently become clear is that validity of self-report is not an all-or-none phenomenon. The degree of validity of self-report depends upon which person is being asked what questions by whom and for what purpose. The questions that are now being addressed in research are "under what circumstances do self-reports vary?" and "how can validity of self-report be enhanced?" (Midanik, 1988). Babor, Stephens, and Marlatt (1987) have suggested that the complex

questioning—answering process is influenced by both task variables
and respondent variables.

Task Variables

It would be imprudent to ignore task variables where offenders are
concerned. Whilst assessment information may be used for intervention purposes, as mentioned at the beginning of this chapter, it may
also be used for reports to court, local review committees, or the
Parole Board. In most cases, offenders are rational people who will
respond to the demands of the assessment situation. It is unrealistic,
therefore, to expect that they will give information which may
increase their chances of a custodial sentence or, in institutions, information which will reduce the likelihood of receiving privileges, parole,
or discharge. The validity of self-report will also be influenced by other
task variables, including the degree of rapport with the questioner,
the extent of confidentiality, and the clarity and complexity of the
task.

Respondent Variables

Offenders may be unable to give valid information for a variety of
reasons. It almost goes without saying that if an offender is intoxicated at the time of assessment then recall will be impaired. Also, conditions pertaining at the time of the offence, particularly high levels
of arousal, may have distorted information processing. The time
interval between the events of interest and assessment may create
problems since by the time legal procedures have been conducted it is
not uncommon to be asking offenders to recall events which have happened some time in the past. During this interval, the fact of giving
numerous accounts of events (possibly not all of them true) to police,
solicitors, and probation officers may have left the offender unsure of
what is fact and what is fiction. In addition to memory decay, the
details in which we are interested may not be those that the offender
attended to at the time.

   Given that these issues will influence the validity of self-report,
how can the professional gather information in such a way that the
likelihood of valid self-report is maximised?

Purpose of assessment. The offender should be made aware of the purpose of the assessment. Whilst clarifying the purpose is no guarantee
of valid self-report, at least the professional and the offender are operating on the same premises. An informed appraisal of whether there

is gain to be made by over-reporting (for example, to gain entry into an intervention programme as an alternative to custody) or under-reporting (for example, to strengthen a case for parole) of both drinking and its relationship to offending will guide the professional in applying some of the other safeguards mentioned below.

Motivation. It is no mistake that this chapter on assessment follows that on motivation: the motivational techniques described in Chapter 5 are essential in maximising the validity of self-report. Firstly, these techniques enable the client and counsellor to build up a rapport. Secondly, the non-confrontational style of questioning minimises the risk of eliciting denial. Finally, in cases where the purpose of assessment is to select a client for intervention, unless a client is at least contemplating change, he or she will see little relevance in providing detailed information about any aspect of his or her behaviour.

Confidentiality. Assuring the client of confidentiality is likely to enhance the validity of self-report (Murray & Perry, 1987); however, it is not always possible to offer offenders complete confidentiality. It is more appropriate, therefore, to describe the limitations imposed by circumstances and to inform the client about who is to be given what information.

Comprehension. Whatever the method of assessment, it is important that questions should be clearly stated so that they are properly understood. Where appropriate, examples should be given to clarify what information is required, for example, with drinking diaries. When using standardised tests, forms should not be issued without first checking that the client can read well enough to complete the task. If questions have to be read aloud, the provision of cue cards for forced-choice answering (for example, "never", "sometimes", "often", "nearly always") helps the client to remember what responses are required.

Aids to recall. Recall of past drinking has been shown to improve if memory cues are provided (Sobell *et al.*, 1988). A calendar, containing both general and personal memory cues, should be drawn up for the period of interest. General cues would be news and sporting events which occurred in that period. Personal cues would be living arrangements at the time, employment, friends and partners, and special events such as birthdays and holidays.

Multiple measures. It is wise not to rely on one source of information and cross-checks on the validity of self-report data become possible when multiple measures are taken (Midanik, 1988). In addition, where a client believes that cross-checks are to be made, validity is likely to be enhanced even if cross-checks are not actually carried out (Murray & Perry, 1987). Other sources of information against which cross-checks may be made are listed below.

Official Records

Official records will contain information useful for corroborative cross-checks. Details of arrests, use of agencies, or hospital treatment may be found, and reports written by other professionals in the past will give some information about the consistency of the client's self-report across time. However, much of the specific detail required in assessment will not figure in official records, for example, quantities and patterns of alcohol consumption.

Collateral Reports

One of the most common ways to check validity is to ask a parent, partner or friend (a collateral) to corroborate a client's self-report. However, it is wrong always to assume that the collateral's report is correct—other people will vary in the extent of their knowledge about the client's drinking. Midanik (1982) suggests that it is tempting to apply the "more is better" principle, where the higher amounts of alcohol consumption and higher rates of alcohol-related problems are taken as valid. If these are given by the collateral, then the client is assumed to be a denier, and if they are given by the client, then the collateral is assumed to be unaware of the true extent of the client's drinking. Nevertheless, the degree of congruence between client and collateral reports does provide some useful corroborative information.

Psychometric Tests

Psychometric tests generally measure what the individual "has" as opposed to what he or she "does" and there are dozens of such tests to measure "alcoholism" or "alcohol dependence". These tests are designed as efficient and economical ways to estimate a construct and may be used to define that individual's current status and to measure changes across time.

Many psychometric tests have serious limitations. Firstly, tests of "alcoholism" or "alcohol dependence" may be problematic because they are designed to measure a construct which is itself flawed.

Arguments against the construct of "alcoholism" have been outlined in Chapter 2. Secondly, a person's test scores mean very little except when compared against those of a similar group of people (a normative sample). Many tests have not been standardised with the groups in which we are interested—in this case British young offenders. Thirdly, where tests are used to measure change across time there may be problems with test reliability: can tests be both reliable and responsive to change? Finally, test results are not useful unless they imply something beyond the score itself, for example which type of intervention is appropriate for this person or how well a person is likely to respond to an intervention. Most tests are limited in this respect.

These problems exist to a greater or lesser degree with all psychometric tests; if selected appropriately and used carefully, however, tests can be valuable assessment tools.

Analogue Assessments

In analogue assessments, a specific situation is created and the client is asked to respond in writing, verbally, or by enacting the scenario in role-play. That is, past events are reconstructed in a simulated setting and the client's responses are observed. The closer the approximation of the simulated situation to the real-life situation, the higher the validity of the analogue assessment.

Analogue methods may include the use of real alcohol to assess drinking behaviour, for example, speed of consumption or resistance to temptation. Rankin, Hodgson and Stockwell (1980) describe a behavioural assessment where subjects were given five vodkas with tonic and the experimenter recorded the time it took the subject to consume the drinks. Those more dependent on alcohol (as judged by a psychiatrist) drank faster than those who were less dependent. In a different paper, the same authors (Rankin, Hodgson & Stockwell, 1983) describe giving two alcoholic beverages to men in an alcohol treatment unit and measuring speed of consumption, subjective ratings of desire to drink, and difficulty resisting a third forbidden drink. These measures were used as a baseline against which to evaluate the outcome of an intervention (cue exposure and response prevention).

Analogue assessments which use alcohol may be of great importance, but they are undoubtedly under-explored due to the ethical and practical difficulties they pose. Most analogue situations involve role-play where the client is asked to demonstrate social skills relating to drinking, for example, assertiveness in saying "No" to peer pressure to drink.

Biological Tests

Tests can be conducted to estimate the presence of alcohol in the blood or urine using non-invasive procedures such as breathalysers and dipsticks. These may be useful in confirming levels of alcohol consumption but are relevant only to drinking that occurred in the previous 24 hours (Leigh & Skinner, 1988). Other tests mainly determine changes associated with liver damage by measuring biochemical markers in the blood. Although these may be of value in detecting chronic alcohol use, they are of limited value when used with relatively healthy people who are heavy drinkers, since the majority will show normal test results (Leigh & Skinner, 1988). Such tests provide little in the way of information about patterns of alcohol use, precipitating factors, and consequences.

Given this range of assessment procedures, which of them may be selected as a useful starting point in assessment of young offenders' drinking and related problems?

SCREENING TECHNIQUES

Screening is a process whereby, on the basis of a relatively simple procedure, a decision is made to select some people for a more comprehensive assessment. To be maximally effective, a screening procedure should not include for further assessment those for whom it is not appropriate (false positives) or exclude from further assessment those for whom it is appropriate (false negatives). No screening procedure will prove to be completely accurate; nevertheless, screening will be essential in some work situations, especially where the professional is dealing with large numbers of potential clients. A screening procedure is described in Chapter 3.

INTERVIEW PROCEDURES

An interview schedule that is designed to access information which may be of importance in understanding a young offender's drinking and its relationship to offending is presented in Table 6.1. The aims of the interview schedule are as follows:

1. to clarify present alcohol consumption levels;
2. to determine the familial and social context of drinking;
3. to identify alcohol-related problems;
4. to examine the relationship between drinking and offending.

This information will contribute to functional analysis and design of interventions, although further information may be required for specific aspects of behaviour.

The interview schedule (see Table 6.1) is divided into three parts: (1) general information; (2) drinking history; and (3) offending history.

Table 6.1 Drinking and offending assessment pro forma

Date of interview .... Interviewer ....
Place of interview .... Purpose of interview ....

A. General Information

1. Name ....
2. Date of birth ....
3. Address ....
   ....
   Own home .... Parent's home .... Tenant .... Other ....
4. Telephone number ....
5. Probation Officer's name ....
                           address ....
                           ....
6. Criminal Records Office (CRO) number ....
7. Family members:
   Relationship   Age
   ....
   ....
   ....
   ....
8. Marital status: Married .... Separated/Divorced .... Single ....
9. Partners: Regular partner ...... Dates frequently ...... No partners ......
10. Who does client live with?
    Name   Age   Relationship
    ....
    ....
    ....
    ....
11. Educational/trade qualifications ....
12. Present employment ....
13. Income ....
14. Employment history
    Job   Duration   Reason for leaving
    ....
    ....
    ....
15. Hobbies/leisure activities ....
    ....

(continued)

Table 6.1   (*Continued*)

B. Drinking History

1. How old were you when you had your first drink? ....
2. Who gave you your first drink? ....
3. How old were you when you began to drink regularly (once every week or more)? ....
4. How old were you when you began to drink heavily? ....
5. In a "typical" week, what do you drink and how much?

	Morning	Afternoon	Evening
Monday			
Tuesday			
Wednesday			
Thursday			
Friday			
Saturday			
Sunday			

Total units ....

6. Where do you usually drink?
   At home ...   Pubs/clubs ...   Friends' houses ...   Outside ...   Other ...
7. Who do you usually drink with?
   Parents ...   Partner ...   Friends ...   Alone ...   Other ...
8. How would you describe the drinking habits of each of the following people?

Mother ...	0 = Abstainer
Father ...	1 = Light drinker
Brother(s) ...	2 = Moderate drinker
Sister(s) ...	3 = Heavy drinker
Partner ...	4 = Problem drinker
Best friend ...	
Yourself ...	

9. What drink-related problems have you experienced? ....
   (a) Relationships ....
   (b) Violence ....
   (c) Finance ....
   (d) Health ....
   (e) Work ....
   (f) Other ....
   ....

Table 6.1 (*Continued*)

10. What do you think caused the onset of your heavy/problem drinking?
....
....

11. Have you ever tried to control your drinking?
Cut down ... Stop ... No ... (If NO, go to Section C)
12. Why did you try to cut down/stop? ....
....
13. How did you try to cut down/stop? ....
....
14. Did you go to anyone for help? If so, who? ....
15. How long did you keep it up? ....
16. What made you return to heavy drinking? ....

C. Offending history

1. Do any members of your family have a criminal conviction? If so, who and for what? ....
....
2. Please list details of your previous convictions:

Offence	Age	Sentence	Relationship to drinking
....	....	....	....
....	....	....	....
....	....	....	....
....	....	....	....
....	....	....	....

3. Current conviction(s) ....
4. Sentence ....
5. Do you think your current offence is drink-related: ....
6. What part did drinking alcohol play in the commission of your current offence? ....
....

7. There are several possible types of relationship between drinking and offending. How strongly do you think these relationships apply to your offending? Please circle a number.

	Always true	Never true
(a) *Drinking is the crime* My drinking is the crime, for example, drinking and driving, drunk and disorderly	1...2...3...4...5...6...7	
(b) *Changes behaviour* Alcohol changes my behaviour, for example, by disinhibition, impairment of judgment, giving courage.	1...2...3...4...5...6...7	
(c) *Causes problems* Drinking causes problems such as over- spending, losing jobs, or arguments with friends or family. These problems lead to crime.	1...2...3...4...5...6...7	

(*continued*)

Table 6.1 (*Continued*)

(d)	*Context* The places where my drinking occurs are where crime is committed or where plans to commit crime are made.	1...2...3...4...5...6...7
(e)	*Crime supports drinking* My crimes are committed to facilitate drinking, for example, stealing alcohol or stealing money to buy alcohol.	1...2...3...4...5...6...7
(f)	*Underlying problems* My personal problems lead to drinking and to crime, and the two are related only through having the same underlying cause.	1...2...3...4...5...6...7
(g)	*Drinking after crime* My drinking comes after the crime, for example, to celebrate or to cope with guilt.	1...2...3...4...5...6...7
(h)	*Excuse* I use my drinking as an excuse for offending	1...2...3...4...5...6...7
(i)	*Increased chance of arrest* My drinking is related to crime only because I am more likely to get caught if I offend after drinking.	1...2...3...4...5...6...7
(j)	*Incapacitation* My drinking is related to a decrease in crime because I am incapacitated, for example, being too drunk to offend or being in a good mood.	1...2...3...4...5...6...7
(k)	*Not related* My drinking and offending are not related.	1...2...3...4...5...6...7

General information

In the first section, information which will identify the client is collected. Since follow-up data will be required, it is important to record means of contacting the client at home or through a probation officer along with relevant official numbers. The client is also asked to describe his or her personal situation relating to family, partners, living arrangements, employment, and leisure activities, since social stability is an important factor in the design and outcome of interventions.

Drinking history

The drinking history section is designed to assess the development of problem drinking in the light of what we know about young people and their drinking. Most young people report having their first drink at around 11 years of age and are typically introduced to alcohol in the home by their parents (Swadi, 1988). As they grow older, they drink more often with friends and extend their range of drinking venues first to parties, then to clubs and discos, and lastly to pubs. Most adolescent drinking occurs at weekends with Saturday being the most popular drinking day.

Population censuses provide data showing the prevalence of alcohol consumption and the typical weekly alcohol consumption for adolescents and young adults (Goddard & Ikin, 1989; Marsh, Dobbs & White, 1986). Male young offenders, by comparison, report drinking far more than their peers in the normative samples, reporting an average weekly consumption of 58 units (McMurran & Hollin, 1989a). These figures are presented in Table 6.2. Guidelines for converting standard drinks into units of alcohol are given in Table 6.3.

Information is also collected about drinking habits of parents, siblings, partners, and friends. Research evidence suggests that children living in a home where a parent has an alcohol problem have themselves a higher chance of developing alcohol-related problems and will also be likely to find a partner whose drinking is problematic (Orford & Velleman, 1991). Peer pressure to drink is also assumed to be an influential factor in controlling adolescent drinking.

As might be expected, heavier drinkers are more likely to experience problems; however, problems occur even at low levels of consumption with light drinkers suffering most illness (sickness, hangovers) and problems with school attendance and performance; moderate drinkers experiencing most interpersonal problems; and heavy drinkers experiencing most legal problems (Werch, Gorman & Marty, 1987). The five main problem areas reported by young

Table 6.2 Prevalence and levels of alcohol consumption

		Age						Young offenders
		13	14	15	16	17	18—24	
Percentage regular alcohol users	Male	29	34	52	46	61	96	88
	Female	11	24	37	36	54	94	
Mean weekly alcohol consumption in units[1]	Male	8.3	11.4	15.9	10.6	16.1	21.4	58.2
	Female	4.7	8.0	9.1	6.2	7.0	8.0	

[1]one unit = one standard drink = 8 grammes alcohol.

Table 6.3   Units of alcohol (1 unit = 8 grammes alcohol)

	Units		
	½ pint, small can or bottle (275 ml)	large can (440 ml)	1 pint
Beers, lagers, and ciders			
3.5% alcohol (ordinary strength beers and lagers; light cider)	1	$1\frac{1}{2}$	2
4.0% alcohol (exports or strong ales; stout)	$1\frac{1}{4}$	2	$2\frac{1}{2}$
5.0% alcohol (continental lagers; ciders)	$1\frac{1}{2}$	$2\frac{1}{4}$	3
9.0% alcohol (special, extra, or super lagers; strong cider)	$2\frac{1}{2}$	4	5
Spirits			
$\frac{1}{6}$ gill (England and Wales measure)	1		
$\frac{1}{5}$ gill (Scotland and N. Ireland measure)	$1\frac{1}{4}$		
1 bottle (75 cl)	30		
Wine			
1 glass	1		
1 bottle (75 cl)	8		
1 litre	12		
Fortified wines			
1 glass	1		
1 bottle	12		

offenders, apart from offending itself, are difficulties with relationships, violence, finance, health, and work (McMurran & Hollin, 1989a); these areas, therefore, are introduced in the interview as prompts for further information.

Offending History

This section contains a checklist of ten possible types of relationship between drinking and offending from which the offender has to select those which apply in his or her case. This adds to the information gained, by asking the direct question "do you think your offending is drink-related?", in that the type of relationship is identified. This is important in that where relationships (a) to (e) apply, reducing levels of alcohol consumption or changing drinking patterns may be expected to reduce crime; however, where relationships (f) to (k) apply, although changes in drinking behaviour may be considered beneficial, a reduction in crime cannot be expected and, in some cases, the likelihood of crime may be increased.

Drinking Diaries

Self-monitoring of drinking behaviour and related events is most commonly done through the use of drinking diaries. Quantity and frequency measures of drinking are always included in diaries and other variables of interest can be included, for example, drinking venues, precipitating events, and consequences of drinking. The advantages of drinking diaries are that self-monitoring relies less on client memory than do retrospective procedures and they should therefore be more accurate; patterns of drinking can be related to environmental events which the client may not have noticed previously; and the client acquires observational skills which may facilitate change (Vuchinich, Tucker & Harllee, 1988).

Self-monitoring is not without problems, however. Some clients will not complete diaries or complete them well after the time drinking took place. It is important to minimise non-compliance by ensuring that the client knows precisely what information is to be recorded, why the information is required, and how it is to be written in the diary. An example of an already completed diary will be useful.

A diary pro forma for one week's drinking is presented in Table 6.4. Diaries may be kept for several weeks so that a picture of the fluctuations in drinking patterns emerges. The quantity—frequency information collected from self-monitoring is also useful in evaluating change during and after an intervention.

FUNCTIONAL ANALYSIS

A wealth of information will be collected during assessment and this must be organised so that the function of the behaviour for the individual can be understood. The background to functional analysis is presented in Chapter 2 and an example of this procedure is presented here.

Example of a Functional Analysis

The details below are taken from an assessment conducted with a

Table 6.4 Drinking diary

Day	Time	Place	Why you started	Who with	Type of drink	Amount drunk	Cost	What happened afterwards
Monday								
Tuesday								
Wednesday								
Thursday								
Friday								
Saturday								
Sunday								

young man who both drank heavily and offended. It should be noted that the example is brief, and that in real life more details would be available. Nonetheless, the example does illustrate the methodology involved in functional analysis. There are various ways of presenting a functional analysis, ranging from complex flow charts to sequential analyses, but to ease comprehension we have chosen to use a simple format here.

The case is that of a young man, referred to as "B", with a history of offences involving fraud and theft. The information used in the functional analysis was gathered from files and from interviews with the young person himself. The analysis is conducted around the drinking behaviour.

Antecedents

B reports an uneven early family life: his mother left home when he was a young child and he was brought up with his brother and sister by his father. His father was violent towards him, administering several beatings (apparently the reason for his mother leaving home), although as he entered his teens he began to assert himself against his father. At this time he began to play truant and made friends with some older boys who introduced him to the pleasures of drinking. As time passed, drinking became an important part of his social life, then simply part of his life so that his drinking grew heavier and heavier. By the age of 19 years, B's drinking had become a serious problem to the extent that he was unable to hold down a job or maintain close relationships with friends of either sex.

Behaviour

Drinking level. B reported a drinking level of 180 units of alcohol per week (1 unit equals $\frac{1}{2}$ pint of beer; 1 measure of spirits). This compares with an average alcohol consumption of 21 units per week among men of his age group in the general population. B scored 35 on the Short Alcohol Dependence Data questionnaire: a score well in excess of the average score (8) on this questionnaire for male young offenders, indicating a high degree of dependence on alcohol.

Drinking pattern. He begins drinking first thing in the morning, keeping two cans of lager on hand for when he awakes. Most of the day is spent drinking, either at home or in a local public house. He drinks both beer and spirits.

Physical reactions. B reports experiencing the shakes first thing in the morning (hence the two cans of lager), he experiences sexual dysfunction in the form of problems in gaining and maintaining an erection, he suffers memory lapses, and has bouts of depression. These physical signs are consistent with high levels of alcohol consumption.

Thoughts about drinking. B sees drinking as having a positive side: it makes him feel happy, cheerful, and funny, helping social interaction. Without drink, the world is a cheerless place, so alcohol helps him conceal his "hurting inside" from the outside world. On the other hand, he recognises that drinking has profoundly affected his life: he is aware of the physical reactions, is dismayed by the lack of close relationships in his life, and recognises the lost educational and work opportunities and the slide into criminal behaviour and prison.

Consequences. The drinking produces rewarding outcomes in that it is a means to social contact, in turn making him feel happy and cheerful. In this sense the drinking is being *positively reinforced* by the social consequences it produces. On the other hand, *not* to drink would produce aversive consequences, some physical in terms of the morning shakes, others in the form of a loss of social contacts and rewards. If the drinking is seen in this way, i.e. to avoid aversive consequences, then this is *negative reinforcement* of the alcohol consumption. This mixture of positive and negative reinforcement is a common pattern in many complex real life behaviours.

To complicate matters still further, the drinking also sets up other negative long-term consequences such as the lack of a job and a steady source of income. This lack of income, in turn, means that money has to be sought illegally to fund the drinking. The criminal offences are a natural progression: if drink is needed, then money has to be obtained by whatever means come to hand.

The case outlined above illustrates how case material can be organised and understood to produce a coherent account of an individual's behaviour. Thus, against a background of family disharmony, not uncommon amongst young offenders, B came to associate drinking with socialisation. Over time the drinking became an integral part of his lifestyle, something which added some positive aspects to his life but at the same time led to some aversive outcomes. The analysis can also be used to begin to highlight some targets for change, particularly in the areas of controlled drinking, skills training in social interaction without the alcohol, and lifestyle modification in holding down a job as well as relationship skills.

Summary

Screening procedures allow identification of clients who may be selected for in-depth assessment (see Chapter 3). An interview with the client gathers information, based on retrospective self-report, about the development of drinking, its social context, and consequent problems. Corroborative information may be gained from official records, and reports from partners, relatives, or friends. For those clients who are at liberty to drink, self-monitoring of alcohol consumption and related events is important in collecting accurate information about drinking patterns. The information collected in assessment may then be integrated into a functional analysis.

Chapter 7

Behavioural Self-control Training

The term "self-control" was originally introduced in the psychological literature as an alternative to "willpower". Both terms may be used to describe a person's ability to resist engaging in behaviours which are rewarding in the short-term but which may be detrimental in the long-term, for example, drinking, smoking, and eating fattening foods. The term "willpower" is, however, typically not used merely to *describe* controlled behaviour but also to *explain* it. For example, a person who has successfully reduced his or her alcohol consumption may be described as demonstrating willpower. Willpower is inferred from our observations that a person no longer consumes large quantities of alcohol, or smokes, or overeats. However, willpower is often then used to explain the observed moderation: how does the person manage to moderate his or her alcohol, tobacco, or food consumption? *Because* he or she has willpower!

Using a construct such as willpower both to describe and explain behaviour is not helpful. This may be seen as an "explanatory fiction": that is, although willpower may at first appear to explain controlled drinking, the reality is that the term is no more than a description of the behaviour. The problems which arise from this way of thinking derive from viewing willpower as a trait: that is, a static, stable characteristic that people have in varying but fixed quantities. The disadvantages of using a trait model of behaviour have already been discussed in relation to motivation (see Chapter 5). To ascribe the observation of control over behaviour—whether it be moderate drinking, quitting smoking, or dieting—to willpower actually stands in the way of both the professional and the client carefully examining the factors which influence behaviour and acting to alter these factors so that the behaviour may be changed in the desired direction.

In using the term "self-control", a different view of behaviour change is encouraged. Self-control is *not* conceptualised as a trait which a person does or does not have in fixed quantities. Instead, self-control may be defined as a set of strategies which an individual can learn in order to recognise and modify the factors that control his or her behaviour. Mahoney and Thoresen (1974) describe this as the individual becoming a "personal scientist": making careful self-observations, collecting and analysing personal data, testing out techniques for self-change, and monitoring outcome. They suggest that people are not accustomed to being systematic in observing their own behaviour and that it may help to teach them to specify the behaviour that requires change, identify its antecedents and consequences, and formulate an action plan.

Kanfer and Gaelick (1986) point out that everyday behaviours can become automatic, that is, their execution is not dependent upon a continual decision-making process. Automatic processing is efficient in that it allows the effortless execution of familiar behaviours. Practised drivers, for example, do not need to deliberate about every manoeuvre they make during a journey and the business of driving is generally facilitated by automatic processing. Where problem behaviours are concerned, an automatic chain of responses triggered by environmental or internal cues is not beneficial and one task of the professional is to "deautomise" troublesome behaviours thus bringing them under control. In controlled processing, unlike automatic processing, attention is focused on the behaviour and decisions are required to be made continually. This frees a person from rigid habitual behaviour patterns and allows greater flexibility in response selection.

Behavioural self-control training, abbreviated to BSCT, is essentially the process of teaching people the skills and strategies required to control their own behaviour. BSCT may be used to pursue a goal of abstinence from alcohol (Hester & Miller, 1987), although it is more commonly applied in pursuit of moderate drinking goals. The techniques include self-monitoring, goal setting, altering the antecedents to drinking, making specific changes to drinking styles, and generating incentives for maintaining change. Use of these techniques may be seen as the responsibility of the client: the professional gives guidance but does not administer the treatment. The techniques are temporary devices, used by the client only until new behaviours become well established. BSCT will be described more fully later in the chapter, but first it is important to examine the evidence for the effectiveness of BSCT.

EFFECTIVENESS OF BEHAVIOURAL SELF-CONTROL TRAINING

Miller (1978) compared three different interventions all designed to reduce alcohol consumption: aversive conditioning (where subjects self-administered electric shocks as they lifted a glass of their favourite alcoholic beverage, took a sniff of its aroma, and imagined sipping it); BSCT; and a combination of the two interventions. At follow-up three months later, all three intervention groups showed significant reductions in alcohol consumption, although the aversive conditioning group was least improved. At this three-month follow-up period, one half of the clients in each group was given a BSCT self-help manual in order to help maintain positive change. After a further nine months, all groups had maintained reduced alcohol consumption and the aversive conditioning group had caught up with the other two groups. Miller attributed this to the positive effects of the self-help manual in those that received it since the manual presented new methods and information to those who had previously received only aversive conditioning.

In each of the above groups, clients who received the self-help manual showed better maintenance of gains than did those not given the manual. The conclusions that may be drawn from this study are that BSCT appears to be effective in reducing alcohol consumption; that aversive conditioning contributes nothing extra to the effectiveness of BSCT and, since there may be objections to this type of intervention on both ethical and practical grounds (it requires electric shock equipment), aversive procedures may be set aside; and, finally, that behavioural self-help manuals may be useful in maintaining reduced alcohol consumption.

From there Miller and his colleagues went on to examine BSCT more closely, finding that BSCT achieved as good a reduction in alcohol consumption when administered with groups of clients as with individually administered interventions (Miller, Pechachek & Hamburg, 1981; Miller & Taylor, 1980) and that self-administered BSCT using a self-help manual worked as well as therapist directed BSCT (Miller & Baca, 1983; Miller, Gribskov & Mortell, 1981; Miller & Taylor, 1980).

Administering BSCT in the form of self-help manuals has been investigated further in the UK, mainly using the commercially available book *Let's Drink To Your Health!* (Robertson & Heather, 1986). Heather, Whitton & Robertson (1986) recruited self-styled problem drinkers from a newspaper advertisement and gave half a behavioural self-help manual and half alcohol education materials. At six-month follow-up, the group which had received the manual showed a greater reduction in alcohol consumption and experienced fewer alcohol-related problems. This improvement was maintained at a one-year follow-up, although the superiority of the group who had received the manual was evident only when those who had received further treatment were excluded from the analysis (Heather *et al.* 1987). A further study of media-recruited problem drinkers showed that people given the self-help manual were less likely to be problematic drinkers at six-month follow-up than were those given an information book, and that offering therapist contact by telephone after receipt of the material made no difference to outcome (Heather, Kissoon-Singh & Fenton, 1990). Further evidence for BSCT being more effective than education, at least in the early stages of an intervention, has been provided by Savage, Hollin & Hayward (1990). Using media-recruited problem drinkers, they presented one half of their subjects first with written BSCT material and then with educational material, and the other half of their subjects with the same material in reverse order: educational material first and BSCT material second. There was greater reduction in alcohol consumption amongst those who received the BSCT component first, suggesting that for those people contemplating change and ready to move into the action stage of change, as defined in Prochaska and DiClemente's (1986) model of change (see Chapter 3), this readiness should be met with techniques for action and that BSCT is appropriate.

To summarise, these studies show that BSCT can be effective in reducing alcohol consumption and may be successfully applied in both individual and group work or by giving the client a self-help manual to work through alone. Hester and Miller (1987) note that the clients who are most likely to benefit from BSCT are those at the lower end of the problem drinking severity continuum, with a shorter duration of problem drinking, lower levels of dependence, and less severe alcohol-related problems. Most young offenders fit this description: they have had relatively short drinking careers and alcohol-related problems, although often serious, are related mainly to intoxication rather than dependence.

BSCT and Offenders

Evidence for the effectiveness of BSCT that is aimed at reducing alcohol consumption in offenders is sparse. However, information about the frequency of use and the helpfulness of specific BSCT strategies is available in a study of young offenders who reported reducing their alcohol consumption without receiving any formal intervention (McMurran & Whitman, 1990).

A list of 35 self-control strategies typically taught in BSCT was presented to 51 male young offenders who claimed to have reduced their alcohol consumption. They were asked if they had used these strategies in their control attempts and, if so, whether they found

Table 7.1 Self-control strategies used by male young offenders (McMurran & Whitman, 1990; reproduced by permission)

Rank order	Strategy	Number of users ($n = 51$)	Number of users who found it helpful
1.	Took up other activities	27	26
2.	Stopped going on pub crawls	23	22
3.	Avoided drinking with people who drink heavily	22	21
4.	Started drinking later	21	20
5.	Stopped buying alcohol to have in the house	20	19
6.	Took less money with me when I went out	21	17
7.	Went to pubs where there was music, pool, darts, etc.	19	18
8.	Treated myself to something nice when I managed to stick to my limit	19	17
9.	Stopped drinking earlier	18	17
10.	Stopped drinking strong or "special" beers	19	16
11.	Stopped drinking spirits	15	15
12.	Calculated how much I spent on drinking	17	13
13.	Set a limit on how much to spend on drinking	15	13
14.	Avoided pubs or clubs where I drink a lot	15	11
15.	Stopped buying rounds	13	12
16.	Changed my drink	14	11
17.	Drank non-alcoholic drinks	12	12
18.	Told my family what I was trying to do	13	11
19.	Set a limit to drinking days per week	12	10
20.	Stopped drinking mixtures, e.g. snakebite	10	9
20.	Took smaller sips	10	9
22.	Told friends what I was trying to do	11	8
23.	Learned the facts about alcohol	10	8
24.	Set a limit to drinks per day	7	6
25.	Stopped holding my glass between sips	8	5
26.	Calculated how much I drank	7	5
27.	Used excuses to refuse drinks	3	2
28.	Timed how long drinks lasted	2	2
28.	Went to someone for help	2	2
30.	Ate a meal before drinking	2	1
30.	Punished myself when I exceeded the limit	2	1
32.	Read books on how to cut down	0	—
32.	Listed the bad things about drinking	0	—
32.	Listed the good things about drinking	0	—
32.	Kept a drinking diary	0	—

them helpful. The strategies were rank ordered, based on the product of the total number of users and the number who found the strategy helpful. The list of strategies is presented in Table 7.1.

This list of strategies should be treated with some caution in that these are the strategies used by young offenders who have successfully controlled their drinking and those who have not managed to do so may have tried these strategies and found them wanting. Also, young offenders may not think of using certain strategies, for example, listing the good and bad aspects of drinking, or reading books on how to cut down: it does not necessarily follow that unpopular strategies are ineffective strategies. This list of strategies does, however, provide information about which techniques are likely to be effective with young offenders and its use should be emphasised in BSCT programmes.

An examination of this list reveals three major groups of strategies and McMurran and Whitman (1990) name specific BSCT techniques in each group that are likely to prove useful with young offenders. The most commonly used group of strategies contains methods of controlling drinking through *social change*, that is, finding alternative activities, avoiding heavy drinking friends, and avoiding situations where heavy drinking typically occurs. Social change may be described as an avoidance of previously heavy drinking social patterns combined with the development of new activities to fill the time that becomes available. These issues will be addressed in the section on rule setting (page 102).

The next most frequently used group of strategies comprises *setting limits*, for example, restricting the days of the week and the times of the day when drinking is permissible, limiting expenditure on drink, and setting a ceiling on the quantity of alcohol that may be consumed in any one drinking session. These issues will be covered in the section on goal setting (page 101).

The third major group of strategies involves *rate control* where, during a drinking session, techniques are employed to ensure that actual alcohol intake (as opposed to overall beverage intake) is held in moderation. These strategies include switching from drinks with a high alcohol content to those containing less alcohol, drinking slowly, and eating a meal before drinking. These strategies will be listed in the section on rate control (page 103).

BSCT IN PRACTICE

The first component of BSCT is *self monitoring* so that information may be gathered about the antecedents to the behaviour, the behaviour itself, and the consequences of the behaviour. From this information, goals for change may be set: that is, there should be aims to reduce alcohol consumption from its initial level and to eliminate offending. Methods of achieving these goals are: firstly, to alter the antecedents through rule setting; secondly, to reduce alcohol consumption through rate control; and thirdly, to manipulate the consequences of drinking through self-administration of rewards.

Since the aim of BSCT is for the client to bring a problem behaviour under self-control, it is important for the professional to apply the programme in a manner consistent with client self-control. The client's responsibility for change can be enhanced by allowing him or her decisional control over the goals that are set, the behaviours to be changed in achieving these goals, and the pace of the programme. Negotiation rather than prescription is essential to this approach (Kanfer & Gaelick, 1986).

The components of BSCT are set out below in order that the professional may assist the offender in the completion of each stage, either in individual interviews or in group sessions. The purpose of each component of BSCT should be stated clearly to the client. There are two main reasons for this: firstly, a person is more likely to comply with instructions where he or she understands the reasons for the request, and secondly, the ultimate aim is that the client should gain the knowledge and skills for behavioural self-control so that these may eventually be applied by the individual without professional assistance. The materials required for BSCT are illustrated in this chapter and should be copied on to index cards or photocopied so that each client possesses a written record of the intervention.

Self-monitoring

There are two purposes of self-monitoring: to collect quantitative information, and to collect qualitative information. Self-monitoring provides an estimate of the quantities of alcohol consumed so that goals for change may be set and change may be monitored over time. Clients may also monitor the antecedents to and consequences of drinking to identify targets for environmental change to reduce the likelihood of drinking or to reduce the likelihood of offending after drinking.

Such information may be gathered using a drinking diary (see Chapter 6), which provides a format for recording all relevant information. Clients should be taught to study their drinking diaries and look for factors which may be associated with heavy drinking and offending—such as the day of the week, the time of day, the places where they drink, the people with whom they drink, activities associated with drinking, the availability of money or alcohol, and the mood they were in before drinking began (Hester & Miller, 1987).

Some clients are unable to keep track of their alcohol consumption and others are unwilling to comply with diary-keeping. Quantitative information may be gathered by asking the client to use a supply of pennies or matches in a frequency count: one penny or match should be moved from one pocket to another for each drink consumed and the total logged after each drinking occasion.

Goal Setting

After monitoring drinking for at least one week, the drinking diary should be studied and goals set. With offenders, two types of goals may be appropriate: reduced alcohol consumption and elimination of criminal behaviour.

In reducing alcohol consumption, limits may be set on (1) the times when drinking is permissible; (2) the amount of money allowed for spending on drink; and (3) the quantity of alcohol consumed in any one drinking session. Where drinking and offending are related, it follows logically to set the second goal of no offending. This serves as a reminder that one negative consequence of drinking is offending and that by adhering to drinking limits the likelihood of offending is reduced.

A statement of these goals should be recorded on a card printed for the purpose, as illustrated in Table 7.2.

Table 7.2 Statement of goals

Drinking limits
Drinking days I will allow myself to drink only on these days of the week:
Drinking times I will not start drinking before _____. I will stop drinking by _____.
Quantity I will not drink more than _____ in any one day.
Money I will not spend more than £_____ on drink in any one day.
Offending I will not commit any of these offences:

Rule Setting (Changing Antecedents)

Offending may be viewed as the culmination of a chain of events, each of which triggers the next. Indeed, in this book drinking is for the most part being treated as one event in the chain that leads to crime. One reason that efforts are being directed primarily at changing drinking is that drinking is a comparatively frequent event when compared with crime and it is therefore easier to examine its antecedents and consequences. An example of a chain of events leading up to crime is as follows: Saturday night is traditionally the night for drinking and dancing in city centre venues and the time of the week triggers off a chain which may involve dressing up, meeting with a group of friends, having several beers in a pub, moving on to a club or disco, drinking several shots of spirits, leaving the club or disco at closing time, milling around with everyone else in the street, and getting into a fight. The easiest way to prevent the fight is to interrupt the chain of events well before the fight erupts. In this example, the offender might be advised to avoid city centre pubs or clubs on a Saturday, change his or her drinking partners, or leave the club or disco before closing time to avoid the melée. Kanfer and Gaelick (1986) refer to this as *decisional self-control* (as opposed to protracted self-control, which is described later): that is, a single choice is made to remove a tempting goal or avoid an aversive situation and, once this choice has been made, it is difficult to reverse.

In interrupting a chain of events we are altering the antecedents so that the undesired behaviour is less likely to occur. These techniques for reducing the likelihood of drinking, known as *stimulus control*, include altering the physical environment, for example, by not keeping alcohol in the house; and altering the social environment, for example, by going out with friends of both sexes rather than drinking in a single sex group. Rule setting is probably the clearest way to teach a person to change the antecedents to drinking and offending. A different set of rules will apply to each person, but they might include restrictions on particular pubs or clubs where heavy drinking is the norm and where fights commonly occur; avoidance of heavy drinking friends and friends with whom offending is most likely; and introducing new activities for times when boredom may precipitate drinking. These rules should be stated in the first person and be quite specific. Examples of rules are:

—"I will not drink in the City Bar."
—"I will not drink with Bill on weekend nights."
—"I will always leave pubs and clubs at least 20 minutes before they close."

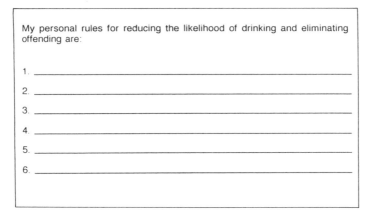

My personal rules for reducing the likelihood of drinking and eliminating offending are:

1. _____

2. _____

3. _____

4. _____

5. _____

6. _____

Figure 7.1   Rule setting

Rules should be recorded in this style for reference using a card typed out for this purpose, as illustrated in Figure 7.1.

Rate Control (Changing Behaviour)

Assuming that many young people will not wish to abstain from alcohol completely, it is important to identify strategies which will help them to control their alcohol intake (as opposed to beverage intake) during a drinking session. Kanfer and Gaelick (1986) describe this as *protracted self-control*, that is, where continued resistance to temptation is required over a period of time. In adhering to limits for reduced alcohol consumption, there are several strategies which may usefully be employed by the drinker. These may be presented as a list of hints for reducing alcohol consumption from which the client may choose those which appeal and to which the client may add others which are relevant to him or her. Hints for reducing alcohol consumption are presented in Table 7.3.

Self-reward (Changing Consequences)

It is important to continue monitoring alcohol consumption to see whether or not limits are being kept, and where limits are successfully kept there should be a reward. Studies of the strategies used by those who attempt to control their drinking without professional help show that the use of self-reward differentiates between problem drinkers who succeed in reducing their alcohol consumption and those who do not (Perri, 1985) and that self-reward is frequently used by young

Table 7.3   Hints for reducing alcohol consumption

1. *Eat a meal before you start drinking*
   Aside from physical problems which may result from drinking on an empty stomach, eating a meal means that alcohol is absorbed into the blood less quickly and so you will feel less drunk and more in control, and if you feel full you will be less inclined to drink large amounts of liquid.
2. *Do not eat salty foods such as crisps and peanuts*
   Salt makes you thirsty—crisps and peanuts are sold in pubs to encourage thirst and increase sales! If you need a snack, have a sandwich instead.
3. *Do not drink alcohol to quench your thirst*
   If you are thirsty, for example, after work or playing sport, drink a glass of orange squash or lemonade to quench your thirst before you have an alcoholic drink.
4. *Switch to a lower alcohol drink*
   Do not drink high alcohol beers or lagers, such as Pils or barley wines or "special brews"—stick to ordinary strength draught beers or lagers.
5. *Choose a low-alcohol drink every other time*
   If you drink beer or lager, choose a low-alcohol brand for every other drink. If you drink spirits, take only the mixer every other time—the tonic or orange juice without the gin or vodka.
6. *Drink half pints instead of pints*
   If you drink pints of beer or lager, take a half pint instead of a pint every other time—pour the half pint into your pint glass if you wish.
7. *Do not drink beer and spirits together*
   It is not necessary to have a measure of spirits along with your beer—stick to one or the other.
8. *Do not drink mixtures*
   Avoid drinking mixed drinks, such as "snakebite" (cider and lager)—these are associated with drinking to get drunk.
9. *Sip your drink slowly*
   You can make your drink last longer if you decide to make each drink last at least half an hour, take small sips, and put your glass down between sips instead of holding on to it.
10. *Do not get involved in buying rounds*
    When people group together and buy rounds of drinks for each other, it is usually expected that each person will buy a round. This means that the number of drinks consumed will equal the number of people in the group. It is easier to keep to a limit if you do not get involved in rounds.
11. *Do not take part in drinking games*
    Drinking games, such as racing your friends to see who can drink a pint fastest or accepting a challenge to drink unusual mixtures, increase your alcohol consumption. Do not participate.
12. *Do not go on pub crawls*
    Moving from pub to pub and having a drink in each one can mean that you drink a lot quite quickly. Unless you are confident that you can stick to low-alcohol drinks, do not join in.
13. *Go to a pub with entertainments*
    If you go to a pub where you can play pool or darts these activities will provide an enjoyable distraction from drinking.

offenders who manage to control their drinking (McMurran & Whitman, 1990). Administering penalties is not used to the same extent and does not appear to be a particularly useful strategy.

When helping a client choose rewards, the following important points should be considered:

1. Rewards may be *material goods*, such as purchase of a tape or disc, a garment, or cosmetics; *special activities*, such as having a late lazy lie-in, going to a rock concert, or spending an afternoon in the gym; or *positive self-statements*, by which the person acknowledges his or her achievements, for example, "I did well" or "I kept to my limit". Whilst novel rewards may be introduced, it is often easiest to rearrange the client's usual self-rewards to make these contingent upon successful goal attainment. It is important that rewards should be realistic: that is, there is no point promising oneself something that is merely a wild dream because it is too expensive or otherwise unattainable. However, some money will be saved by reducing drinking and this can be reserved to purchase a special treat. But remember, rewards should never be alcoholic drinks!
2. Rewards should be tailored to individual preferences: that is, we

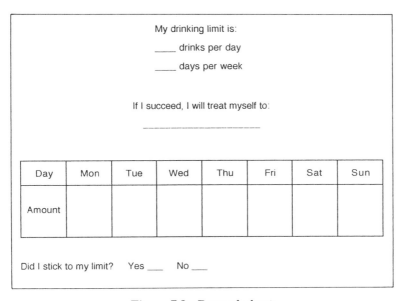

Figure 7.2 Reward chart

all enjoy different things and so what constitutes a reward will vary from person to person.

3. Rewards should be identified at the start of the period to be monitored so that the behaviour is targeted at earning these rewards, and administered immediately at the end of that period.
4. Rewards should vary across time to prevent satiation.
5. Rewards may be set daily or weekly at first, then the period to which they apply may be extended gradually, perhaps by working towards a larger material reinforcer. Eventually, the artificial structure of incentives should be abandoned altogether.

A record of successes and failures, along with nominated rewards for that period, may be kept on cards printed as illustrated in Figure 7.2.

METHODS OF APPLYING BSCT

It has already been mentioned that BSCT has proved effective in reducing alcohol consumption when applied in three different ways: therapist-directed intervention with individuals; therapist-directed group intervention; and through the use of self-help manuals by the client. The choice of method of application may depend on resources, for example, whether the professional has time for individual work with clients or whether finance is available for the purchase of self-help manuals. Although resource issues cannot be ignored, there are other factors important to the choice of method. Issues relevant to selection for group interventions and individual interventions are addressed in Chapter 3. The use of self-help manuals requires the consideration of specific issues.

Although it may seem obvious, it is important to ensure that any client offered a self-help manual is sufficiently literate to be able to make use of the material. Literacy is not, however, the only criterion for selecting clients for a self-help manual intervention: a willingness to accept this form of intervention is important. Where a client is reluctant to receive a self-help manual, he or she may not read the book at all or may read only parts of it, and the resulting incomplete application of the intervention may have no effect on drinking or may even exacerbate the problem (Barrera, Rosen & Glasgow, 1981). Where a manual is given, it is essential to check with the client in a follow-up session the extent to which the manual has been used and the effects the programme has had.

Self-help manuals do, however, offer some advantages. Firstly, manuals can be offered to offenders for whom no other form of intervention is available, for example, those held in prisons where there are no trained alcohol counsellors. Secondly, in institutions where alcohol is not available, the client cannot practise self-control strategies and so presenting the information in written form gives the client possession of a programme which he or she may apply at a later date when required. Thirdly, self-help manuals are an economical intervention, cheap relative to professionals' time, and, if they prove effective in reducing alcohol-related offending, cheaper by far than legal and penal costs. Recommended commercially available self-help manuals are listed in the List of Resources section.

Summary

BSCT is the process of teaching a client systematically to monitor and modify his or her behaviour. The strategies involved are:

1. Self monitoring: through the use of drinking diaries, information is gathered about the antecedents to drinking, the drinking behaviour itself, the consequences of drinking.
2. Goal setting: limits to drinking are set by restricting the times when drinking is permissible, expenditure on drink, and level of alcohol consumption allowed in any one drinking session.
3. Rule setting: environmental and social changes are encouraged by setting rules for altering drinking contexts and promoting alternative activities to fill the time that becomes available.
4. Rate control: strategies for reducing alcohol consumption (as opposed to beverage consumption) are introduced.
5. Self-reward: new contingencies are introduced to maintain controlled drinking.

Chapter 8

Social Skills Training

Like most other animals, humans are social creatures. The smooth functioning of our world depends upon being able to communicate with other members of our species. We need to be able to inform other people of our wishes and intentions; and we need to be receptive to the feelings of other people. The ability to communicate is vital to every sphere of our life that involves other people. We have to communicate with our family and friends, with colleagues at work, with casual acquaintances—in short, with just about everybody we meet. Clearly it is in everyone's best interest that we have a communal language to ease smooth social communication. *Verbal communication*, that is, the spoken (and written) language, is one way in which we pass information among ourselves. However, again like most other animals, humans have developed a highly sophisticated means of passing information that relies upon *non-verbal communication*.

THE ELEMENTS OF SOCIAL SKILLS

Non-verbal Communication

An understanding of non-verbal communication is central to the topic of social skills training and hence an overview is given below. More expansive coverage can be found in Argyle (1975; 1983) and Knapp (1978). The research evidence on non-verbal communication highlights several discrete ways in which we both send and receive non-verbal messages.

Bodily contact. This is perhaps the most primitive of social acts and is found in many species, including humans. The act of touching can convey many messages—an aggressive push, a loving caress, a consoling pat, a friendly handshake, or a thump on the back in good humoured congratulations. However, when it comes to touching there are strict social conventions to observe. These social conventions dictate which parts of the body it is permissible to touch in different relationships, say, between mother and son and father and daughter, or friends of the same sex and friends of the opposite sex. While it seems that females touch more than males, there are also vast cultural differences in both the frequency and intensity of touching. To touch or be touched oneself is a very strong communication—when we observe other people touching each other we can usually infer a great deal about the type of relationship or nature of the interaction between those involved.

Gesture and posture. Technically, *gestures* are movements of any part of the body that convey some message to onlookers. However, in practice the term is most often used to refer to movements of the hands, arms, and head. Common gestures include a wave of greeting, an opening outward of the palms of the hands to indicate puzzlement, or a nod of the head to signify agreement or understanding. Some gestures have become highly sophisticated, as for example with "tick-tack" sign language used by bookmakers at a racecourse, or the formal sign language used by people with impaired hearing.

The term *posture* refers to the way in which we hold our bodies. A distinction is often made, for example, between a "closed" posture and an "open" posture: in the former the sitting person typically has crossed legs and folded arms in a tense and anxious manner; in the latter the person has arms apart and legs uncrossed in a relaxed manner. We can both convey and read emotions quite easily using posture: we are able to recognise a range of emotional states as indicated by, for example, an aggressive posture, a submissive posture, or a frightened posture. As well as posture, *bodily orientation* is also important. We face towards those with whom we wish to communicate, but turn our backs on those we ignore; more subtly, the angle at which we face each other is important—a "face on" orientation between two men indicates a quite different type of interaction as would be the case with the same orientation but between members of the opposite sex.

The face. The face contains a great deal of socially important information; indeed, facial expression conveys the most basic emotions—fear, anger, happiness, surprise—in a way that most people can readily understand. Changes in facial expression are also used for facilitating social interaction, for example, our frowns and smiles indicate our approval and disapproval as we listen in conversation. Eye movements, as in gaze and eye contact, can have effects quite out of proportion with the physical effort involved. A glance across a crowded room can have all sorts of consequences! Eye contact and length of gaze are highly potent means by which to signal intent: extended gaze and prolonged eye contact can indicate great interest and a willingness to initiate further interaction of either a hostile or intimate kind. There are also conventions regarding the length and duration of eye contact appropriate to both speaker and listener in conversations.

Appearance. This term is generally used to refer to the artificial aspects of non-verbal communication. This includes such social signals as clothing, hairstyle, jewellery, and cosmetics.

Verbal Communication

The analysis of verbal communication, especially conversation, is highly complex although such analysis is of undoubted relevance to social skills training (Argyle, 1986; Coulthard, 1984; Good, 1986). Speech, of course, serves several functions: it may be used to ask questions; to pass information; to give opinions; to direct the thoughts and actions of other people; or to deliver praise and rebukes. However, as well as the spoken word, there are also those aspects of speech that do not involve language, referred to as *paralanguage*. Examples of paralanguage include the use of silence, as to indicate disapproval, and "hesitation pauses" in which the speakers gather their thoughts. Voice qualities can also convey information about the speaker: volume, tone, pitch, and regional accent say as much, if not more, about the speaker than the meaning of what is being said.

Learned Social Skills

While there are many variations on the theme of the non-verbal "micro" behaviours as discussed above, it is important to note that these behaviours should complement each other in two ways. Firstly, each person uses their individual skills in a co-ordinated manner, so that their eye contact, posture, gesture, and speech mesh in a uniform fashion to maximise their chances of successful communication. Secondly, the passage of communication between people should ebb and flow in a regulated manner: rather like two proficient tennis players, those involved in social communication should, as dictated by the rules of the game, move both to make their shot and to anticipate the return signalled by their opponent's movements. Thus the micro behaviours of verbal and non-verbal communication form complex amalgams of "macro" behaviours—social skills such as being assertive, holding a conversation, or attending a meeting—that are needed to function effectively in everyday life.

Argyle and Kendon (1967) put forward the idea that social behaviour, comprising both micro and macro behaviours, can be thought of in the same way as motor skills such as typing a letter or driving a car. In developing this analogy, Argyle and Kendon suggested a basic model, shown in Figure 8.1, by which to understand the notion of social skills.

Goal. Like the car driver who, at certain times of the week, might have the goal of driving safely between home and work, each person has social goals that he or she wishes to achieve. There are many social goals, such as having friends, maintaining a long-term relationship, being successful at work, and being liked by certain people. Social goals are probably a product of basic human needs such as affiliation and achievement as defined and valued by various cultures and sub-cultures. However, the achievement of social goals demands that the social situation is created in which the goal can be pursued. The car driver whose garage entrance is blocked is unable to enter the road traffic system that will allow the goal of driving to work to be attempted. Thus there are many social situations—meetings, parties, conversations, interviews, and so on—that we encounter every day,

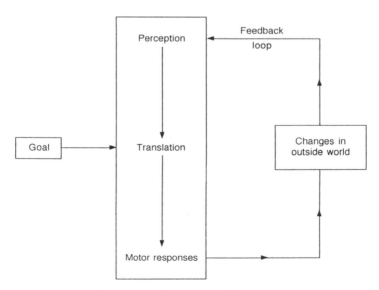

Figure 8.1 The social skills model

and each offers an opportunity to achieve some social goal. Rather like the highway code, there are *social rules* that apply to different social situations: as our driver would drive in a different way on a motorway than on a crowded high street, so the socially skilled person will behave in a different way at a funeral than he or she would at a party. Social rules serve a number of functions: they allow a constant flow of communication; they seek to avoid high levels of aggression and subsequent physical harm; they co-ordinate behaviour among those with a common interest; and they can help to promote co-operation between those with similar goals.

It is also the case that, for whatever reason, some social situations are generally seen as difficult. Furnham and Argyle (1981), studying mainly the views of young people, found several distinct clusters of social situations that commonly caused difficulties. These types of difficult situations are shown in Table 8.1.

Inspection of these problematic situations suggests that they are characterised by *unfamiliarity*, so that the social rules are unclear; or by *complexity*, so that they make heavy demands on attention and ability; or by *formality*, so that any mistakes will be instantly identified by other people.

Perception. The car driver needs to learn the meaning of the various signals that will guide his or her actions. During a single car journey the driver will encounter road signs, road markings, traffic lights and

Table 8.1   Difficult social situations (after Furnham & Argyle, 1981)

Assertiveness
   Complaining to a neighbour about a noisy disturbance
   Taking an unsatisfactory article back to a shop

Intimacy
   Taking a person of the opposite sex out for the first time
   Visiting a doctor when unwell

Counselling
   Going round to cheer up a depressed friend
   Going to a close relative's funeral

Public performance
   Giving a short speech
   Being host at a large party
   Going for a job interview

Parties, etc.
   Going to a function with many people from a different culture
   Attending a wedding

warning lights; there will be other cars on the road and sometimes cyclists and pedestrians, even the odd stray dog. All this information alerts the driver that immediate action is needed, or that he or she might need to take a certain course of action; alternatively, the signs might simply give the driver a progress report, say how far they have to go to reach their destination. In the same way as the car driver, we are surrounded by social signals and messages in the form of non-verbal and verbal communication. The socially skilled person is aware of which messages to attend to, what the messages mean, and how to respond to stay on course to achieve social goals and avoid collision with the other people involved.

Translation. What we perceive we "translate" into action: the messages from the world around us must be evaluated and considered to decide on the best course of action. The motorist who sees the lights changing to red can decide to either accelerate to move through before the change is complete, or slow down in anticipation of the change. A number of factors may influence this translation stage: being in a hurry to get to one's destination or a clear road ahead might translate into a decision to speed up; a busy road or a police car might translate into a decision to slow down. In the same way, we must translate social signals into action: we need to consider the options open to us in a given situation, weigh up the likely consequences of these different options, then make the best decision to suit our own interests and those of the other people involved. Of course, not every situation requires careful scrutiny and evaluation; we meet some situations and people so often that our actions become automatic or habitual and so do not require deep contemplation. Indeed, if we had to think our way through every situation as if we were meeting it for the first time life would be very slow. Experienced and skilful people can quickly negotiate their way through most situations without too much conscious strain.

Responses. After perceiving the environmental signals and deciding upon an appropriate course of action, the final part of the sequence demands a repertoire of skilled behaviour to allow the desired response to be made. The motorist must, for example, be able to steer the vehicle, co-ordinate clutch, accelerator and brake, and be able to operate the lights, windscreen wipers and other instruments. Socially skilled people must also have command over both their verbal and non-verbal behaviour to co-ordinate the various elements of these communication skills and so produce appropriate sequences of complex behaviours.

Feedback. The eventual response will, in turn, have an impact on the outside world: other people will react favourably or unfavourably, accidents will or will not occur, goals may be achieved or missed. Perceptually capable people will be able to adjust their responses as they perceive and translate the effects of their actions. Thus the feedback indicates that their response was effective, and therefore that similar actions may be appropriate at that instant; or that some corrective manoeuvre is required. This feedback will also inform future behaviour should a similar situation be encountered. The inclusion of a feedback loop in the social skills model emphasises that social behaviour, like driving, is not a static process: our behaviour is constantly changing and shifting as the situation and the people who are part of it changes; in turn the situation changes because of the impact of our behaviour.

Social Skills Training

If conventional social behaviour can be understood with reference to the model outlined above, then it follows that abnormal social behaviour can be explained in terms of a breakdown at any of the three stages of perception, translation, or response. Trower, Bryant & Argyle (1978) note several ways in which a breakdown in social skills can occur. Social perception skills may be dysfunctional so that, for example, there are low levels of discrimination and accuracy in perceiving interpersonal cues; or there may be systematic perceptual errors, such as constantly seeing others as aggressive. Errors at the translation stage may be evident in a failure to consider alternative courses of action, or continually to make poor or negative decisions; or to fail to learn the appropriate rules for different situations. Finally there can be shortcomings at the response stage of the model: there can be difficulties with discrete elements of social performance such as eye gaze or facial expression; and problems with more global aspects of social performance such as being assertive or holding a conversation.

Now, if disturbances in social behaviour are to be understood by reference to this model, does that have any implications for clinical work? Argyle (1967) was quick to spot the potential: "Some psychiatric patients might be treated by training in social skills: this would cure those symptoms which consist of disturbances of social behaviour, as well as others that result from it" (p. 18). Argyle's suggestion was to go on to provide the impetus for the development of the technique of social skills training. However, before looking at the application of social skills training with offender groups and with problem drinkers, the next step is to consider the assessment and training methods typically used in social skills training.

Assessment

There are three areas to consider in the assessment of social skills: (1) goal assessment; (2) situational assessment; (3) skills assessment.

Goal assessment. The content and focus of social skills training should be dictated to a large degree by the goals the trainee wishes to achieve. Of course it may be that the client's goals are contentious in that they are dangerous, undesirable, immoral or even illegal; in addition, the client's motivation for change and ability to give a rational account must also be taken into consideration. While the goals are usually negotiated before training is begun, allowance should be made for some modifications as training progresses.

Situational assessment. Trower, Bryant & Argyle (1978) devised the Social Situations Questionnaire, shown in Table 8.2, which allows the trainee to specify the types of social encounters he or she finds difficult. The trainee can, for example, make judgments—such as "no difficulty", "slight difficulty", "moderate difficulty", "great difficulty", or "avoid if possible"—about each situation; or can make frequency ratings—such as "every day", "at least once a week", and so on—to indicate how often the problem occurs. Of course, one should not be bound by a questionnaire; careful interviewing may well reveal other situations that a particular trainee finds problematic.

Skills assessment. Researchers and practitioners have developed a variety of assessment methods by which to gauge an individual's social skills. Assessment methods for social perception skills include recognition of non-verbal cues from photographs and drawings; or involving the trainee in observing and describing a videotaped social interaction to determine if they have the ability to detect fine nuances of social behaviour. As discussed in Chapter 2, cognitive assessment poses special problems, however assessment methods for translation skills have been developed: these include measures of problem solving ability and various self-rating scales in which the client offers an opinion as to the areas that he or she finds particularly difficult or problematic. The assessment of response skills is well developed, drawing on traditional behavioural methods such as observation and role-play (Becker & Heimberg, 1988). In a typical assessment procedure, the client might be asked to role-play a particular scene. This

Table 8.2 Social situations questionnaire (after Trower, Bryant & Argyle, 1978)

Situation	No difficulty 1	Slight difficulty 2	Moderate difficulty 3	Great difficulty 4	Avoid if possible 5
			Rating		
1. Walking down the street					
2. Going into shops					
3. Going on public transport					
4. Going into pubs					
5. Going to parties					
6. Mixing with people at work					
7. Making friends of your own age					
8. Going out with someone you are sexually attracted to					
9. Being with a group of the same sex and roughly your age					
10. Being with a group containing men and women roughly your age					
11. Being with a group of the opposite sex of roughly your age					
12. Entertaining people in your home, lodgings, etc.					
13. Going into restaurants or cafes					
14. Going to dances, dance halls or discotheques					
15. Being with older people					
16. Being with younger people					
17. Going into a room full of people					
18. Meeting strangers					
19. Being with people you don't know very well					
20. Being with friends					
21. Approaching others—making the first move in starting up a friendship					
22. Making ordinary decisions affecting others (e.g. what to do together in the evening).					
23. Being with only one other person rather than a group					
24. Getting to know people in depth					
25. Taking the initiative in keeping a conversation going					
26. Looking at people directly in the eyes					
27. Disagreeing with what other people are saying and putting your own views forward					
28. People standing or sitting very close to you					
29. Talking about yourself or your feelings in a conversation					
30. People looking at you					

role-play is observed, even videotaped, by the trainers and note made of the strengths and weaknesses of the client's response skills.

Skills Training Methods

The methods used in social skills training have been described in many texts (e.g. Trower, Bryant & Argyle, 1978; Wilkinson & Canter, 1980). The most frequently used training methods are described below.

Modelling

The modelling or demonstration of a particular skill or element of behaviour, either "live" or by use of videotape, has several advantages. Modelling can illustrate and magnify important components of a task to facilitate learning; it can set standards for the trainee to aim for; and it can serve as the basis for further practice. With modelling, particular attention should be paid to the characteristics of the model: strong learning is best served when the model is of similar status to the trainee.

Rehearsal

While learning can take place through observation of a model, it is undoubtedly true, especially with complex skills, that rehearsal and practice are necessary to achieve high levels of performance. A typical training sequence, therefore, might involve the trainer in modelling a skill such as attentive listening; followed by the trainee practising in a role-play what he or she has observed about attentive listening. Not all rehearsals should take place within the confines of role-play. The use of "homework" tasks, through which the client is able to practise new skills in more realistic settings, is also important for effective training. There is a positive relationship between the amount of practice and skill acquisition: more practice leads to better skills.

Feedback

While modelling and rehearsal are important, feedback that provides information on performance, both in role-play and real life, is crucial for good skill acquisition. Feedback guides the trainee towards making an accurate appraisal of his or her performance. Feedback is given through observation of videotaped role-play sequences followed by verbal discussion of performance. Of course, many clients find this a rather stressful experience in the early stages of training, and so it is helpful to be as constructive as possible when giving feedback. It is all too easy when giving feedback to be negative and focus on errors. Try to adopt an approach that first identifies what went well; then ask questions of the type "how do you think you performed?" and "if you were going to do it again, what might you change to make it even better?"

In practice, feedback typically takes two forms: *intrinsic* feedback refers to the individual's appraisal of his or her own actions; *extrinsic* feedback comes from other people such as the trainer or other members of a social skills group (or, in the natural environment, from other people). While extrinsic feedback is important, the goal in training should be to fade out this type of feedback and build up intrinsic feedback. The goal is therefore to help the trainee to become proficient at monitoring and accurately appraising his or her performance. Thus time spent in discussion assisting the client to appraise accurately their performance is clearly time well spent.

Reinforcement

As noted above, at the beginning many trainees find social skills training difficult and stressful. For this reason a reinforcement system will both encourage trainees to persevere and will ease learning. The reinforcement may simply be praise for participating in training; alternatively, a tangible reward for participation and progress might be advantageous in some cases. In the long run, however, it is the attainment of the desired social goal that will provide the necessary reinforcement.

In total, these training methods can be applied to each type of skill acquisition—perception, translation, response—as detailed in Table 8.3.

Generalisation

If trained skills are to generalise to the real world and so allow trainees to achieve their goals in the context of their social networks, then training should be structured to this end. The training course must be tailored to the needs of the trainee: for example, some individuals may benefit from group training, while others will be better suited to individual work; equally, some trainees are able to learn quickly, but others may have learning difficulties. In addition there are various strategies—such as training in the real world and drawing relevant people into training sessions—that can be used to facilitate generalisation following skills training (see Brown, 1982; Huff, 1987).

Table 8.3 Skills and skills training methods

Perceptual skills
  Verbal guidance
  Recognition practice
  Feedback

Translation skills
  Verbal guidance
  Discussion

Response skills
  Modelling
  Role-play
  Feedback
  Verbal and visual guidance

SOCIAL SKILLS, DELINQUENCY, AND ALCOHOL

Once the technique became established, social skills training became immensely popular and it has been put to a variety of uses. Social skills training programmes have been devised for clinical populations such as schizophrenics and depressives; for the professional training of medics, teachers, and managers; and for "everyday" events such as adolescent problems and marital and relationship difficulties (Hollin & Trower, 1986a; 1986b; 1988). In this widespread application of social skills training, both delinquents and heavy drinkers have been (as separate populations) targeted for skills training. The use of social skills training with these two populations raises three issues: (1) what is the basis for the use of social skills training?; (2) what has been the focus of the training programmes?; (3) has the use of social skills training been successful?

Social Skills Training with Delinquents

Why Choose Social Skills Training?

The use of social skills training with any client group implies that members of that group experience difficulties of some type in social interaction. Is there any evidence that delinquents have particular social skills problems?

With regard to social perception, the evidence is severely limited. In the only published study of social perception with a delinquent sample, McCown, Johnson & Austin (1986) found that, compared to non-delinquents, the delinquents could recognise the facial expressions of anger, fear, and happiness equally well, but were less able to detect sadness, surprise, and disgust. Moving on to translation skills, several studies have suggested that young offenders experience some difficulties with this particular aspect of social ability. For example, Freedman, Rosenthal, Donahue, Schlondt & McFall (1978) found that young offenders gave fewer competent solutions than non-offenders to a series of social problems contained in the Adolescent Problem Inventory. In particular, the delinquents used a more limited range of alternatives than the non-delinquents to solve interpersonal problems, and relied more on verbal and physical aggression. Another study by Veneziano and Veneziano (1988) used the Adolescent Problem Inventory to subdivide a sample of delinquents into three groups: those who were incompetent in their knowledge of social skills, those who were moderately competent, and those who were competent. The least competent group experienced more behavioural difficulties generally than their more competent peers. Similar results have been found with female delinquents (e.g. Ward & McFall, 1986). Finally, Spence (1981) compared the social performance skills of 18 male young offenders with 18 non-delinquent males, matched for age, academic ability, and social background. The delinquent group was rated by observers as less socially skilled than the non-delinquents.

Social Skills Training Programmes

The force of much of the research discussed above is that delinquents do have social skills difficulties. However, before looking at a typical programme, two important points must be made: (1) the range of evidence in support of any relationship between social skills and delinquency is limited; the most recent review (Henderson & Hollin, 1986) identified only 20 studies and few have been reported since; (2) there are individual differences *within* delinquent populations—it would be a mistake to assume that all young offenders will experience social skills problems. Notwithstanding these points, a number of social skills training programmes for young offenders have been designed. A timetable for a typical social skills training programme is shown in Table 8.4.

In keeping with the theory discussed previously, the social skills training programme as detailed in Table 8.4 first sets individual social goals for each trainee. These goals are typically, but not always, concerned with delinquent activities such as getting involved in fights, dealing with police and other authorities, and dealings with delinquent peers. The resolution of family difficulties is another common goal and skills training programmes have been designed specifically for this goal: Serna, Schumaker, Hazel & Sheldon (1986) present a model programme to teach reciprocal social skills to delinquents and their parents. Following goal setting, the "micro-skills" of non verbal communication are then followed by training in more complex, "macro-skills"; these complex skills are then applied in training sessions designed around the trainees' goals. As will be discussed later, the outcome studies have revealed some important findings regarding the effectiveness of social skills training with young offender populations.

Table 8.4 Timetable for a typical social skills training programme with delinquents

The social skills training course consisted of ten 90-minute sessions held at the rate of one per week. The basic structure of the course is given below:

Session 1: Introduction to social skills training methods; first exposure to videotape and demonstration role-plays. Trainees to agree on personal aims and objectives to be achieved from the course.

Session 2: Relaxation training, leading to posture, leading to non-verbal communication (NVC) in full: eye contact, facial expression, personal space, gestures, etc. Emphasis on the importance of NVC in impression formation.

Session 3: Verbal skills: listening and talking skills. Blend with NVC for competent social performance.

Session 4: Verbal skills continued: development of conversational skills; "ice break"—use of appropriate topics to instigate conversation in a variety of social settings.

Sessions 5—9: Application of social skills as taught above to trainees' specific problems. Included were sessions on job interviews, interactions with prison and aftercare staff, confrontations with police officers, conversation with members of the opposite sex, handling aggressive encounters with peers.
    A typical example was the session led jointly by a police officer from the local juvenile bureau. The officer, familiar with skills training techniques, assisted in the enactment of various incidents the trainees had experienced with police officers. After role-play of the original incident, training in how better to manage similar incidents was given using the police officer's skill and guidance. The most common incidents were being stopped in the street for questioning and being called on at home.

Section 10: Overview of course, final points answered. Post-course evaluation.

Note: After C. R. Hollin and M. Henderson (1981). The effects of social skills training on incarcerated delinquent adolescents. *International Journal of Behavioural Social Work and Abstracts*, 1, p. 148.

Social Skills Training with Problem Drinkers

Why Choose Social Skills Training?

As with deliquency, we begin with the same starting point for problem drinking: is there any evidence that problem drinkers have particular social skills difficulties?

Historically there is a long-standing association between social competence and alcoholism: studies such as those reported by Sugarman, Reilly & Albahar (1965) and by Levine and Zeigler (1973) suggested that there was a strong relationship between heavy drinking and low levels of social ability. In a typical study, Braucht, Brakarsh, Folungstad & Berry (1973) found that adolescent problem drinkers were aggressive, lacking in personal control, and too impulsive. Once confirmed as a heavy drinker, the young person is liable to form friendships with other young people who are also heavy drinkers. This, in turn, may lead to a variety of further problems, some caused by being part of a drinking culture, others stemming from being labelled "anti-social".

Once the pattern of experiencing difficulties with social situations is formed, from the micro level of judgment of facial expressions of emotion (Borrill, Rosen & Summerfield, 1987) to forming and maintaining long-term relationships with peers, then various further problems can develop. It may be that the skills to deal effectively with complex social situations are never acquired; or that, when such skills are acquired, some social situations engender such high levels of anxiety that the skills to function effectively are inhibited. In either case alcohol may offer an effective means of *coping* with difficult social encounters. Indeed, the use of alcohol may be made more likely by the *expectation* that it will make it easier to cope with difficult social situations.

Several studies have identified the types of social situation commonly experienced as problematic by heavy drinkers. Some studies, reviewed by Monti, Abrams, Binkoff & Zwick (1986), have shown that problem drinkers have difficulties in social situations that demand assertive behaviour. This is most strongly evident in situations that are stressful in that they bring about strong feelings: thus, in summarising the research work of Marlatt (see Chapter 9), Monti *et al.* comment that "A combination of a negative emotional state plus the inability to express oneself effectively can lead to an increase in alcohol consumption" (p. 117). It will be recalled that social situations demanding assertive behaviour are generally one of the most demanding types of situation (see Table 8.1). There are, of course, other reasons for drinking: alcohol can facilitate social interaction, and it has obvious properties in changing perception and sensation (e.g. Sturgis, Calhoun & Best, 1979). Therefore, before embarking on a skills training programme it is important to determine each trainee's motivation for drinking in order to design a relevant programme.

Social Skills Training Programmes

To help with the assessment of problematic social situations, Chaney, O'Leary & Marlatt (1978) devised the Situational Competency Test for use with problem drinkers. (It is interesting to note the similarities between this test and the Adolescent Problem Inventory discussed previously.) As Chaney (1989) notes, this test can be administered in several ways: by talking through the situations— either live or by tape recording—and then recording the trainee's responses; by pencil and paper presentation and recording; or by a combination of pencil and paper and tape recording. Trainees are asked to imagine themselves in a given situation and then describe what they would say or do given those circumstances. These situations are selected to reflect "high risk" situations in which there is an increased likelihood of drinking. The Situational Competency Test contains 16 situations in all; typical examples are shown in Table 8.5.

Of course, the full range of social skills assessment methods should also be used (see above) along with situational measures to give as full a picture as possible of the trainee's current strengths and weaknesses.

Armed with the assessment results, a social skills training

Table 8.5   Examples from the Situational Competency Test (after Chaney, 1989)

You have taken your car to be repaired and the mechanic gave you an estimate. When you return to pick up your car, you find that the bill is for twice as much as what the mechanic told you before and is much more than you think it should be. What do you do?

You are at a big family party. You are being careful not to drink even though almost everyone else is drinking. A relative who knows you have a drinking problem comes over. He says "Why not have a couple of drinks with the rest of us and then quit? Just one or two won't hurt." What do you say to him?

You've been feeling lonely lately, but the only friends you can think of getting in touch with are your old drinking buddies. You give one of them a call. He starts to invite you out for a drink. What do you say to him?

programme can be designed to help the trainee achieve his or her goals. There are a number of typical goals in social skills training with problem drinkers: managing those situations (usually demanding assertive behaviour) that can produce frustration and anger if not managed effectively; coping with negative personal feelings such as loneliness and boredom; and managing situations in which there is social pressure to drink. As Monti *et al.* (1986) note in their review of the field, there has been a substantial number of social skills training programmes reported in the literature.

Guided by the situational assessment, the focus is therefore on training skills to help cope with stressful social demands. Chaney (1989) has described the useful strategy of taking a problematic situation and formulating a response guideline to foster effective coping and so avoid drinking. Two examples are shown in Table 8.6; however, it should be possible to construct similar personalised guidelines for any situation that a trainee describes.

Table 8.6   Skills training strategies for problem drinkers (after Chaney, 1989)

Situation
During the last few months your drinking problem has kept you from holding onto a job. You are now interviewing for a job and the interviewer says "It doesn't look like you have been able to stay with a job very long lately."
Response
You want something the other person has control over. To get it, you need to impress the interviewer that you are in control of your actions. Therefore, handle the implied criticism directly by explaining that you have had a drinking problem and that is the main reason for your unemployment. Don't get trapped in lies. Mention that you are going through an alcohol treatment program and indicate what your employment goals are.

Situation
You go to a party with a date. He or she appears to ignore you during the course of the evening. You are on your way home and feel hurt because of his or her behaviour.
Response
You want to change the way you feel. Check your perception of the situation with the other person. Express what you feel ("I feel..."). Ask the other to clarify what he or she is saying so that you are sure you understand his or her point of view. State where you agree and disagree about what he or she has said and how it has made you feel. Try to reach agreement on the reasons for the situation. Share the responsibility. Stay on the topic. Compromise. Step back from the situation if necessary. Try to see the other person's point of view, but don't lose sight of your own needs. State what you will and will not do in response to his/her request and how you would like to see his/her behaviour toward you change in the future. Agree on a specific course of action that you feel OK about, which will remedy the situation or prevent its recurrence.

Through the training of appropriate non verbal and verbal communication skills, the trainee can be helped to gain improved assertion skills, conversational skills, drink refusal skills, and self-management skills to cope with negative feelings. The aim of such programmes is, of course, to help the trainee achieve social goals without the need for heavy drinking. In the next section we turn to the question of outcome—how effective is social skills training in achieving the desired outcomes?

The Effectiveness of Social Skills Training

Delinquency

Social skills training programmes with delinquents have been evaluated in many ways—see Hollin (1990) for a more detailed discussion. Several investigators have been concerned with the minutiae of social behaviour, such as eye contact and tone of voice: the outcome evidence with delinquents is positive in showing that delinquents are capable of making substantial improvements in such micro behaviours after social skills training. Another means to assess the effectiveness of social skills training is by monitoring changes in performance on complex social tasks. Again the outcome evidence is positive in showing that delinquents are able to improve considerably in, for example, handling conflict with their parents, resisting peer pressure, and improving institutional behaviour. At a third level, some studies have looked at the long-term effectiveness of social skills training in terms of its effects on offending. While the evidence is somewhat limited, there is no compelling reason to believe that social skills training has any impact on criminal behaviour.

Drinking

As with delinquency, a range of strategies has been used to evaluate the outcome of social skills training with problem drinkers. There is sound experimental evidence to indicate that social skills training with problem drinkers can increase ability in micro behaviours such as improved speech fluency and other elements of non-verbal communication. In addition, there is strong evidence both to suggest that improvements in macro skills such as assertion and managing frustration can also be achieved and that these positive changes improve performance in those situations assessed as problematic by measures such as the Situational Competency Test. Finally, and crucially, there is evidence to suggest that improvements in social skills can reduce drinking. While there are some reservations and the success rate is by no means perfect, there are grounds for optimism: Monti *et al.* note that social skills training can "Contribute to improvements in patients' social effectiveness and help problem drinkers reduce drinking" (p. 129); while Chaney (1989) concludes that "Skills training has received sufficient empirical validation to be ensured a permanent role in alcoholism treatment" (p. 219).

Summary

Is there a role for social skills training with young offenders who drink heavily? We have seen that social skills training has little, if any, impact on offending, but that it can have a significant impact on reducing drinking and preventing relapse. To address this issue we need to reconsider the lessons discussed in Chapter 2 regarding functional analysis.

If we look first at the lack of evidence for recidivism we have to ask the fundamental question—why should we expect social skills training to reduce offending? This expectation rests on the assumption that there is a *functional* relationship between social skills deficits and problems and offending, and that by changing social skills the offending behaviour will be reduced accordingly. However, while there is some evidence to suggest that some, but not all, delinquents may experience social skills problems, there is little evidence to show that poor social skills are a cause of criminal behaviour. It follows that the expectation is false, given the present state of knowledge, that social skills training will have any impact on offending (Hollin & Henderson, 1984).

However, for drinking, the position is quite different: there is good evidence that some, but again not all, heavy drinkers experience social difficulties. These social difficulties have been linked in a theoretically cogent manner with problem drinking, and social skills training programmes have been devised to address precisely those problem social situations related to heavy drinking. Further, the positive outcome evidence regarding the effects of social skills training on drinking supports the efficacy of this approach in helping to cut down drinking.

In order therefore to conduct successful training programmes there are several key points to remember:

1. Social skills training is effective in improving social ability both in terms of micro and macro skills.

2. Social skills training can be effective in helping problem drinkers reduce their drinking.
3. It is highly unlikely that social skills training will reduce offending *unless* it can be shown that there is a functional relationship between social skills and offending.
4. For young offenders with drink problems, social skills training will only therefore have a chance of being successful in reducing offending if it can be shown that there is a functional relationship between the drinking and offending.

Chapter 9

Relapse Prevention

In attempting to change drinking behaviour there is an undeniable problem to be faced: that of high rates of relapse. That is, clients often manage to control their drinking temporarily but have difficulty entering into the maintenance stage of change (see Chapter 3). Because relapse is a common phenomenon in all the so-called addictive behaviours, it has received considerable attention from clinicians and researchers, leading to the intervention programme known as relapse prevention. This programme is designed to teach people who are attempting to change their behaviour to anticipate and cope with situations that might precipitate a relapse (Marlatt, 1985a).

Before relapse prevention techniques are described, it is important to clarify what is meant by relapse. The term "relapse" is, perhaps, an unfortunate choice in that it derives from the disease model and implies a return to illness from a state of cure or remission. In fact, much of the research into relapse is based on the disease model of "alcoholism" where abstinence is the "cure" and to have even one drink is a "relapse". If abstinence is the goal and to have a single drink is considered a relapse, then the high relapse rate found in outcome studies may paint an unnecessarily pessimistic picture of the possibility of long-term change (Larimer & Marlatt, 1990). Where moderation is the goal, relapse has a different meaning which depends on how moderation is defined. Any definition of moderation will include limits on the quantity of alcohol consumed and the frequency of drinking occasions, and will include a reduction in the number of alcohol-related problems, including offending. The limits that are set and the problems that are avoided will vary from client to client, yet it is in terms of these goals that relapse must be defined. Larimer and Marlatt (1990) suggest that relapse should be defined in terms of an individual's goals, with a single violation of the goals being construed as a lapse or a slip, and relapse being a return to the previous levels of consumption and/or an abandonment of the change attempt.

This definition allows some flexibility in approach which may benefit the client. Where relapse is defined in terms of the client's goals for moderation, there are no longer only the two mutually exclusive positions of abstinence and relapse, which, as Marlatt (1985a) points out, creates the risk of any violation of abstinence leading to a full-blown relapse. Although some clients will aim for abstinence, they, as well as those aiming to moderate their consumption, may benefit from distinguishing a "lapse" from a "relapse". Lapses may be seen as limited events which need not become uncontrolled relapses. Opportunities are thus created for investigating the situational and psychological factors which lead to lapses and so jeopardise successful maintenance of change, and for developing strategies for coping with these risk factors.

Relapse prevention is based on the identification of those situations in which the client is at high risk of relapse into heavy drinking, and teaching skills and strategies for coping with these high-risk situations. Marlatt (1985b) lists eight common determinants of relapse in two main categories: intrapersonal and interpersonal. These are listed in Table 9.1.

Table 9.1 Classification of determinants of relapse (after Marlatt, 1985b)

A. Intrapersonal determinants
1. *Unpleasant emotions*
   Experiencing frustration, anger, loneliness, boredom, worry, and other negative emotional states.
2. *Physical discomfort*
   Experiencing alcohol-related discomfort such as withdrawal, or other discomfort which is not related to drinking, such as pain, illness, and fatigue.
3. *Pleasant emotions*
   Feeling happy, excited, pleased, and other positive emotional states.
4. *Testing personal control*
   Wishing to test one's ability to engage in moderate drinking to see what happens.
5. *Urges and temptations*
   Feeling a "craving" for alcohol, or unexpectedly finding oneself in a drinking situation, such as a visitor calling with a bottle or finding some drink in a cupboard.

B. Interpersonal determinants
1. *Conflict*
   Having arguments, disagreements, or fights with other people.
2. *Social pressure*
   Being urged to drink by others, or seeing people drinking and feeling the need to join in.
3. *Pleasant times*
   Drinking to enhance pleasant times, such as a romantic or sexual situation, a night on the town, or a celebration.

Of these situations associated with high risk of relapse, unpleasant emotions, interpersonal conflict, and social pressure are those which account for most relapses, but different people find different situations problematic. Annis (1990) has identified two relapse profiles: the high negative profile and the high positive profile. People with a high negative profile are more likely to drink in response to situations involving unpleasant emotions and conflict with others, drink alone, have a high level of alcohol dependence, and be female. Those with a high positive profile are more likely to drink in response to situations involving positive emotions, drink with others and respond to social pressure to drink, have a low level of alcohol dependence, and be male.

Recent findings in smoking cessation research suggest that different types of relapse determinants may prevail at different stages in the change process. Craving may pose the highest risk in the early days, but craving attenuates as times goes by and risks are then related more to positive social situations and times of pleasure and celebration. The highest risk factors in the later stages of the change process, before maintenance is reached are negative emotions and situations, which may operate as excuses for relapse (Velicer, DiClemente, Rossi & Prochaska, 1990).

This information about common determinants of relapse will help in the assessment of an individual's high-risk situations for drinking. Once risks have been identified, the coping skills required for relapse prevention can be taught. Annis (1990) defines the goal of relapse prevention as "to enhance client self-efficacy in all identified areas of drinking risk" (p. 120). According to self-efficacy theory (Bandura, 1977b), maintenance of behaviour change depends upon the extent to which the client believes he or she will be able successfully to cope in a high-risk situation. When a high-risk situation is encountered, the client will appraise the situation in terms of past experiences, present personal, interpersonal and environmental factors, and available coping strategies. This will lead to a judgment by the client of his or her ability to cope (an efficacy expectation), which will determine whether or not heavy drinking occurs. That is, knowing what skills may be used for coping in high risk situations is not sufficient for those skills to be successfully employed: a person must also believe that he or she can actually apply these coping skills in that situation and that, when applied, they will work. Relapse prevention aims to enhance self-efficacy so that coping skills are more likely to be applied effectively, thereby reducing the likelihood of drinking.

Although the aim is to introduce cognitive change—that is, a change in the way an individual appraises a situation—the methods of effecting change are based on activity rather than discussion.

Observation, rehearsal, and real-life experience of mastery in high-risk situations are worth hours of verbal persuasion. The components of relapse prevention include identification of high-risk situations, teaching skills for coping with temptation, covert modelling of coping responses, teaching skills for coping with lapses, and graded practice. These components will be described more fully later in the chapter, but first it is important to examine the evidence for the effectiveness of relapse prevention.

IS RELAPSE PREVENTION EFFECTIVE?

In a study by Allsop, Saunders and Carr (cited in Allsop & Saunders, 1989), 60 men in an alcohol treatment unit were randomly allocated to one of three conditions: (1) a cognitive—behavioural relapse package; (2) a relapse discussion group; and (3) no intervention control. The two interventions were additional to the unit's programme and were conducted in eight one-hour sessions; the no intervention control group received no additional relapse-prevention training.

The cognitive—behavioural relapse package was performance-based and comprised motivational interviewing, identification of high-risk situations, problem-solving training, teaching methods of coping with lapses, graded practice, and reviewing reasons for decisions to change. The relapse discussion group was, as the name suggests, discussion-based and participants examined past relapse experiences, considered potential high-risk factors, and discussed strategies that might minimise relapse.

At a six-month follow-up, more of the subjects who had received the cognitive—behavioural package showed improved self-efficacy ratings compared with the discussion and control groups, and fewer had relapsed to heavy drinking. The post-intervention self-efficacy rating was the best predictor of outcome at six months, compared with dependence measures, initial alcohol consumption levels, and measures of cognitive functioning. These findings suggest that relapse prevention is effective in reducing the likelihood of return to heavy drinking; that performance-based interventions are superior to verbally mediated ones; and that self-efficacy is associated with positive outcome.

Annis, Davis, Graham and Levinson (cited in Annis & Davis, 1989) studied 83 employed "alcoholic" clients who had completed a three-week inpatient alcohol programme. They were randomly assigned to either relapse prevention or supportive counselling, both on an out-patient basis and both conducted in eight sessions over a three-month period. High-risk situations for each client were assessed using the Inventory of Drinking Situations (Annis, 1982) and clients were categorised as having either a generalised profile, where all kinds of situations appear equally to precipitate relapse, or a differentiated profile, where there is greater risk in some types of situation than in others. At six-month follow-up, only clients with differentiated profiles who had completed the relapse prevention training showed a lower level of typical daily alcohol consumption. These results suggest that relapse prevention is more effective than supportive counselling for those clients who are able to identify specific high-risk situations.

Relapse prevention techniques have also been applied with smokers (Shiffman *et al.*, 1985), dieters (Sternberg, 1985), and illicit drug users (Stallard & Heather, 1989). Another major area of application which will be dealt with at greater length in the following section is relapse prevention with sexual offenders.

RELAPSE PREVENTION WITH OFFENDERS

Outcome studies of relapse prevention in controlled drinking programmes are still relatively few and none describes its application specifically with offender populations. Relapse prevention has, however, been applied with sexual offenders, directed at controlling their offending behaviour *per se*.

Sexual offending has been likened to an "addiction" in that there are commonly features of compulsion and loss of control, and relapse—or recidivism—rates are high. Marques and Nelson (1989) note also that the most frequently observed determinants of relapse to sexual offending are the same as those for relapse to heavy drinking, namely negative emotional states and interpersonal conflict. Because of these similarities between sexual offending and "addiction", relapse prevention has been adapted for use with sexual offenders. Pithers, Marques, Gibat and Marlatt (1983) describe such a relapse prevention programme in full, and a long-term evaluation comparing recidivism rate in a treated group of offenders with that of a prison only control group is currently underway. Although results are not yet available, sexual offenders who have received the relapse prevention programme express confidence in its potential for helping them avoid reoffending (Marques & Nelson, 1989).

McMurran (1991b) describes a cognitive—behavioural intervention with a 20-year-old imprisoned rapist, comprising sex education, social skills training, and relapse prevention. The relapse prevention component included explanation of the control as opposed to cure rationale; identification of high-risk situations; rule-setting; identification of apparently irrelevant decisions; teaching strategies for coping with urges; covert modelling of coping responses; and reviewing reasons for decisions to change. Self-control was measured using the Thorne Sex Inventory (1965) with the score indicating an improvement in self-control immediately after the intervention and still further improvement at one-year follow-up. Two years after the intervention, and one year after release from prison, the young man had not reoffended and he reported a balanced lifestyle of further education, various social activities, and a regular girlfriend.

For a fuller description of relapse prevention with sexual offenders see Laws (1989).

TECHNIQUES OF RELAPSE PREVENTION

Coping Versus Cure Rationale

In setting the scene for assessment and relapse prevention, the rationale for these procedures should be explained to the client: that is, that the intervention will provide methods of coping with high-risk situations, but it cannot be expected to make such situations disappear altogether.

Marlatt (1985c) describes reliance on an addictive behaviour pattern as a means of exercising control over natural emotional reactions, particularly negative ones. This control is, however, illusory, and control over emotions is actually *lost* in the use of an addictive behaviour. Marlatt (1985c) likens this loss of control to being literally lost and uses the analogy of a map in finding a sense of direction. The map provides information about the path that has led one to the present location and the route that one must follow, avoiding dangerous terrain, to reach one's chosen destination.

The process of change may be translated into the metaphor of a journey. The most important stage is preparation for the trip, including identifying one's present location (self-monitoring); choosing a destination (goal setting); predicting potential problems (identification of high-risk situations); and selecting the necessary equipment for the journey and learning how to use it (skills training). During the journey, it is important to consult a map to keep on the right track and avoid dangers and dead-ends (avoidance of high-risk situations) and, should problems be encountered, to deal with them and resume the journey (coping with temptations and lapses).

Assessment of High Risk Situations

There are four sources of information about determinants of relapse: questionnaire, accounts of past relapses, drinking diaries, and descriptions of relapse fantasies. In each case, the situations under scrutiny are those where the client drank more than he or she wished, or where personal drinking limits were exceeded. As already stated, there is no prescribed definition of what constitutes a relapse since this will depend on each client's individual goals.

Questionnaire

The Inventory of Drinking Situations (Annis, 1982) is a 100-item questionnaire designed to assess situations in which the client drank heavily over the past year. Based on Marlatt's (1985b) classification of determinants of relapse, it contains examples of each of the eight types of high-risk situation. The client is asked to estimate the frequency of "heavy drinking" (according to his or her own definition) when in each of the various situations during the past year. Responses are collated to provide a client profile showing the greatest areas of risk.

Accounts of Past Relapses

The client should be asked to recall previous situations where he or she drank more than intended. It is important to examine specific relapse events, not occasions of heavy drinking in general. That is, after listing previous relapses, each one should be examined separately and the client prompted in remembering specific details such as the day of the week, the situation in which drinking occurred, who else was present, what events precipitated the drinking, and feelings experienced before drinking began.

Drinking Diaries

Drinking diaries are useful in examining recent situations where the client has exceeded his or her drinking limits. For each relapse event recorded in the diary, prompts should be given as above to elicit the required information.

Relapse Fantasies

People who are attempting to change their behaviour often imagine or

Table 9.2 Checklist of determinants of relapse

Brief description of relapse event ....
....
....

A. Intrapersonal determinants	Present	Absent
1. Unpleasant emotions	...	...
2. Physical discomfort	...	...
3. Pleasant emotions	...	...
4. Testing personal control	...	...
5. Urges and temptations	...	...
B. Interpersonal determinants		
1. Conflict	...	...
2. Social pressure	...	...
3. Pleasant times	...	...

dream of indulging in the proscribed behaviour. Descriptions of these fantasies and dreams can provide clues about the determinants of relapse.

The information collected from each of these three sources should be aimed at identification of the determinants of relapse listed in Table 9.1 above. In examining events from accounts of past relapses, drinking diaries, and relapse fantasies, determinants of relapse can be recorded on a checklist, as illustrated in Table 9.2. After several check-lists have been completed, the information contained in these should then be collated to produce a hierarchy of high-risk situations: that is, the determinants should be listed in order of frequency of occurrence. This serves two purposes: firstly, the client is made aware of situations that present the highest risk for relapse; and secondly, the relative priority of coping skills training becomes apparent.

Assessment of Coping Skills and Self-efficacy

There are two factors involved in successfully coping with high-risk situations: knowing what coping strategies to use, and having the belief in one's ability to use these coping strategies effectively (self-efficacy). Having drawn up a hierarchy of determinants of relapse, the next step is to assess the client's repertoire of coping responses and perceived self-efficacy in applying these coping responses. There are three methods of collecting this information: questionnaire, self-report, and role play.

Questionnaire

The Situational Confidence Questionnaire (Annis, 1987) is a 39-item questionnaire designed to assess self-efficacy in alcohol-related situations. Clients are asked to imagine themselves in a variety of types of situations and rate how confident they feel in their ability to resist the urge to drink heavily in each situation. Responses on the Situational Confidence Questionnaire allow the counsellor to monitor changes in self-efficacy ratings over the course of an intervention.

Self-report

A series of hypothetical high-risk situations can be presented to the client as an exercise in eliciting coping responses. These vignettes should be relevant to the client; closely approximating to the situations in which relapse has previously occurred or to those in which the client suspects that relapse is likely in future. Examples of vignettes of high-risk situations are presented in Table 9.3.

Self-efficacy in each of the coping strategies reported can be assessed by asking the client to state how confident he or she feels in being able successfully to execute the coping strategy in that

Table 9.3   Hypothetical high-risk situations for coping skills assessment

1. "It is Thursday evening and you had a date to go out with your boyfriend; however, he phoned you at 6 pm to say that he had the opportunity to work overtime and so he wanted to cancel your date. You were angry with him and you had a big argument over the phone. Now you are at home alone, feeling bored and sorry for yourself. How would you cope with this situation?"

2. "You spent Saturday afternoon visiting your father and just as you were about to leave he gave you some money to spend on yourself. Your plan was to go home and change before meeting your friends in the bar at 9 pm. Now you have this extra money and it is only 7 pm. What do you do next?"

3. "You are in the bar with your friends and when you ask for a pint of orange squash they begin to make insulting remarks, such as 'Pete thinks he's an alcoholic!' and 'Pete can't hold his drink!' What do you do in this situation?"

4. "Tuesday evening is a time you have set aside for doing something which doesn't involve drinking. You have decided to go to the cinema. On your way there you meet some friends who are heading for a nearby bar. They invite you to join them. They seem to be having a lot of fun. What do you do in this situation?"

particular situation: very confident, fairly confident, moderately confident, not very confident, or not at all confident.

Self-report information may be obtained in interview or in written form. As a written exercise, this may be given to clients to complete in their own time between sessions. For clients who cannot or prefer not to write, the same material can be presented on audio-tape and responses recorded.

Role-play

A high-risk situation may be simulated in role-play and the client's performance scored either by an observer or by video-taping the role-play for review later. In a role-play assessment, the professional would score performance firstly by noting the final outcome (successful or unsuccessful); secondly by counting the number of statements and actions that could be helpful in avoiding relapse; and finally by asking the client to rate his or her level of confidence in being able to cope with the situation in real life.

Coping with temptation

First of all, it is important to advise the client that he or she can expect to feel the desire to drink from time to time, particularly in high-risk situations, and that this should not come as a surprise. Marlatt and George (1984) point out that, when people feel the discomfort of an urge or craving, there is a tendency to assume that the discomfort will continue to mount until resistance collapses under the strain. However, since urges and cravings are triggered by environmental or internal cues, their duration is, in fact, limited. These feelings of discomfort may be likened to waves which swell to a peak and then subside. Coping with urges and cravings is like surfing, that is, riding the swell until it disappears.

When a desire to drink does occur, this should become a cue for activating coping strategies.

Positive Self-statements

Self-statements should remind the client that the desire to drink was expected, that the desire need not be acted upon, and that the desire will disappear given time. Relevant self-statements are:

—"I expected to feel like having a drink and it's not that bad really."
—"I feel like having a drink, but I don't need to have a drink."
—"I feel like having a drink, but I won't let the feeling beat me."

Decision Review

Commitment to change is likely to be enhanced where the person keeps in mind the reasons that prompted the initial decision to change (Saunders & Allsop, 1989). One strategy which serves to do this, and also acts as a delaying tactic after recognising a desire to drink, is to review the reasons for deciding to cut down. This may be done using a decision matrix, as illustrated in Figure 9.1, on which the client may record the likely positive and negative consequences of drinking and not drinking, both in the short-term and the long-term.

In completing this matrix, the client will be reminded of the positive consequences of not drinking, for example, maintaining a good relationship with one's partner, being efficient at work, or feeling in

	Immediate consequences		Delayed consequences	
	Positive	Negative	Positive	Negative
Not drinking				
Drinking				

Figure 9.1 Decision matrix

control, and the negative consequences of drinking, for example, offending, financial problems, or hangovers. This should strengthen resolve to adhere to reduced drinking goals. In addition, the positive consequences of drinking, for example, relaxation, socialising, or feeling "high", and the negative consequences of not drinking, for example, boredom, having to stay at home, or worrying about one's problems, suggest to the client what issues should be addressed to make resistance to temptation easier.

In identifying both immediate and delayed consequences, the client is encouraged to address what Marlatt (1985a) calls "problems of immediate gratification", or the PIG: that is, the tendency to concentrate on the initial effects at the expense of long-term physical health and social well-being.

Distraction

Although it is useful to recognise the desire to drink, make positive self-statements, and review one's reasons for deciding to change, a time limit should be placed on these strategies. That is, it may be counterproductive to concentrate for too long on one's desire to drink and distraction becomes the better option.

The best distracting activities are incompatible with the behaviour one is trying to control, for example, swimming is a good alternative activity because it is impossible to swim and drink at the same time (not counting chlorinated water!) However, it is difficult to think of many activities which totally exclude the possibility of drinking: in going for a walk in town there may be a bar passed en route; the sports centre where you do weight training may serve alcohol; if you decide to cook or bake, the recipe may demand a splash of sherry or brandy.

In choosing alternative activities, it is important to be on the look out for "seemingly irrelevant decisions" or SIDs. These are choices which on the surface appear to be distractions from the desire to drink but actually place a person in a situation of greater temptation. Marlatt (1985a) suggests that seemingly irrelevant decisions may, in fact, be covert plans to relapse. Examples of seemingly irrelevant decisions might be: the choice of visiting a friend where the friend is known to be one who usually offers drinks to guests; the decision to do the weekly shopping in the supermarket where the drinks section must be encountered during the journey through the aisles; or the decision to go out for a meal or a snack and choosing a bar as the place to eat.

Cue exposure

One specific type of high-risk situation is simply being in the presence of alcohol and related environmental cues. There is evidence to suggest that environmental cues for drinking, such as the sights, sounds and smells of a bar, through repeated pairings with actual alcohol consumption, may themselves in time acquire the ability to elicit craving for alcohol. Cue exposure is a technique for attenuating this link between environmental cues and craving. Essentially, cue exposure is based on the assumption that it is possible to correct this conditioned craving by repeated exposure to drinking cues without allowing alcohol consumption to follow.

One question that this raises is what may be defined as a cue? Laberg (1990) mentions the obvious cues such as bottles, glasses, and bar surroundings, but cautions that these may not be the cues that make the greatest impact. Cues which elicit conditioned craving may be altogether more complex, such as being in a particular context whilst in a particular mood and having had a moderate amount to drink. For example, a young offender may feel a stronger desire to drink heavily in a city-centre bar with his friends on a Friday night after having consumed one or two beers than he will when in a local bar with his father having a drink before Sunday lunch.

Rankin, Hodgson and Stockwell (1983) applied cue exposure techniques with problem drinkers by allowing them to drink two alcoholic drinks then pouring a third which they were asked to resist. Over the next 45 minutes, subjective ratings of desire to drink and difficulty in resisting were taken. Over the course of six cue exposure sessions, all subjects drank their two priming drinks progressively more slowly and there were significant decreases in ratings both of desire to drink and difficulty in resisting. Cue exposure interventions such as this are still relatively rare in the alcohol field, possibly due to the belief that alcohol ought to be completely avoided by the problem drinker, although this is clearly unrealistic for most people (Heather & Bradley, 1990). To neglect the issue of cue-related craving may be to ignore an important determinant of relapse.

Theoretical issues relating to the mechanism by which cue exposure has its effects are currently under debate. It is not yet clear, for example, whether cue exposure serves to extinguish a conditioned response or to enhance beliefs about self-efficacy (Laberg, 1990; Marlatt, 1990). Given the theoretical uncertainty, it may be prudent to employ procedures that combine extinction and skills training.

Hodgson (1989) suggests that problem drinkers should be exposed to pubs, parties and the taste of alcohol, firstly, so that coping skills can be practised in the face of temptation; secondly, so that conditioned responses to environmental cues can be extinguished; and thirdly, so that self-efficacy beliefs can be enhanced. McMurran (1991a) recommends the use of a simulated bar setting in conducting interventions for young offenders with alcohol-related problems where cue exposure would play its part as skills training occurs.

Covert Modelling

Covert modelling is a technique where the client is asked to imagine encountering a high-risk situation and engaging in a coping response. This technique is useful in situations where skills cannot be practised in real-life situations, or where it is difficult to set up a sufficiently realistic role-play, for example, in working with prisoners.

After identifying high-risk situations, a script is prepared for each of them. The script should be a detailed description of a high-risk event which the client has encountered in the past or expects to encounter in the future. The client should provide the details for this script, including information about the setting, the people present, what is said, thoughts, feelings, and actions. The script is then prepared as a story which will be read aloud to the client so that he or she can mentally act out the situation which concludes with the client coping successfully.

Prior to reading the script aloud to the client, a state of muscle relaxation should be induced. Instructions for muscle relaxation are presented in Chapter 10. An example of a covert modelling script is as follows.

It is Friday evening. You have decided to go to the bar with your friends but you do not want to drink too much. Imagine yourself entering the Bourbon Street Bar with John and Dave. You can hear the buzz of conversation and the music in the background. The atmosphere is warm and smoky. You go to the bar for drinks.

You have decided that the best way to stick to your limit is to buy your own drinks. If you get involved in rounds, there will be pressure to drink at the rate of the fastest drinker in the group. You want to enjoy yourself, but you do not want to get drunk.

John offers to buy the first round. He says, "What are you having?" You feel apprehensive about opting to buy your own drinks because the others might see this as unsociable, but you state your case. "I'll buy my own drinks tonight, thanks. It may seem a bit unsociable, but I want to cut down my drinking and this is the easiest way for me to do it." You feel pleased that you have been able to say this.

John says, "Oh, come on! You've got to join in. You can't sit there all night with one beer like an old man!" You feel uncomfortable at John's remark, but you hold out. You say "It may seem boring, but I definitely do want to cut down my drinking. I'll just buy my own so that I can drink at my own speed." You turn away to go to the bar for your drink. You hear Dave whisper, "Asshole!" You decide to ignore him.

You order your drink from the barman. You feel pleased that you have opted out of the round. You pay for your drink and rejoin your friends. You begin a conversation. Your plan has worked and now you are in control of your drinking for the whole evening. You will not get drunk, you will not overspend, and you will not get into a fight. You will still have a good time with John and Dave. You feel pleased that you have succeeded.

A covert modelling script should be *personal*, in that it is written and spoken in the second person; *specific*, in that particular bars and people are mentioned; and *realistic*, in that it must contain scenes and vocabulary with which the client is familiar. The script should contain detailed information about the coping strategy, describing specific actions and verbal responses. There should also be emphasis on the good feelings that result from using these strategies effectively.

Coping with lapses

In relapse prevention, it is important to acknowledge that setbacks may occur and teach the client skills for coping with these. Marlatt and George (1984) liken this to a procedure such as a fire drill, which prepares us to cope with a dangerous situation should it arise. Fire drill training does not, however, give us permission to start a fire, nor does it increase the likelihood of a fire occurring, but it does minimise the danger should an accident occur.

The essence of coping with setbacks is to avoid the "goal violation effect" (GVE) or the "abstinence violation effect" (AVE). These are similar processes which apply to violation of moderation and abstinence goals respectively. The abstinence violation effect is the description given to the observed behaviour that when a lapse occurs this often leads to a full-blown relapse, for example, a dieter who eats one chocolate biscuit may not stop at one but go on to consume the whole packet! Marlatt (1985c) suggests that when people who fail to keep to their limits attribute their lapses to internal stable causes, such as lack of willpower, they will feel unable to regain control, and that the state of dissonance engendered by wishing to adhere to drinking limits yet feeling powerless to do so creates the condition where the drinker is likely to amend these conflicting views by giving up the controlled drinking goal. Together, the two processes of internal attribution for failure and reduction of dissonance between the ideal state (adherence to goals) and actual state (violation of goals) increase the likelihood of a lapse becoming a relapse.

Marlatt (1985c) proposes that, in the early stages, violation of personal goals should be defined as a lapse or a slip rather than a relapse, and that the likelihood of a goal violation effect should be reduced by encouraging the client to attribute the cause of the lapse to external, changeable, and specific factors, for example, encountering a high-risk situation. External attributions are less likely to lead to feelings of conflict; that is the drinker is not perceived as someone who wishes to cut down but does not have what it takes to do so, but rather is someone who is trying to cut down but has yet to render difficult situations controllable through the application of coping skills. Where feelings of conflict are minimised, resolution of conflict through cognitive appraisal of oneself as a "lost cause" becomes less compelling, and the likelihood of the goal violation effect is consequently reduced. The lapse may then be studied to identify what conditions triggered the undesired behaviour and to formulate plans for coping with similar situations in future.

It has been pointed out that empirical support for the goal violation effect and the abstinence violation effect is limited (Allsop & Saunders, 1989), and that, in fact, very little is known about how lapses become relapses. However, it is important in practice to attempt to weaken the link between lapses and relapses (Shiffman, 1989), and the strategies for this are: cognitive reframing, formulating emergency procedures, and relapse rehearsal.

Cognitive Reframing

The "one drink then drunk" maxim of Alcoholics Anonymous carries with it the risk of creating a self-fulfilling prophecy: a person who takes one drink may then see getting drunk as inevitable and so do nothing to avoid it. To prevent relapse, the client should be encouraged to view a lapse as a single event occurring at a specific place and point in time. That is, just because one drink has been consumed, it is not necessary to continue to drink the whole bottle; or just because one evening was spent drinking and getting drunk, there is no need to do the same the next evening.

The client should be advised that, since drinking is a behaviour that has developed over time, bringing rewards in certain situations, it is not surprising for lapses to occur now and again in the early stages of change. Marlatt (1985c) recommends that lapses should be reframed as learning opportunities instead of failures, teaching the client about the high-risk situations to which he or she is vulnerable.

```
A lapse is not a relapse

1. Stop drinking
2. Put your glass down
3. Remind yourself of your reasons for deciding to
   cut down/stop drinking
4. Leave the high-risk situation
5. Do something else that you like
```

Figure 9.2   Emergency procedures

Emergency Procedures

When a lapse occurs, it is important that the client should have a readily available list of strategies to apply immediately so that one drink does not become two drinks, or two drinks become three, and so on. A list of emergency procedures may be devised in consultation with the client and recorded on a reminder card, as illustrated in Figure 9.2, for quick reference at the time of the lapse.

Relapse Rehearsal

Relapse rehearsal is covert modelling with a different emphasis: the client is asked to imagine that a lapse has occurred and to rehearse coping skills that will limit the lapse, preventing it from becoming a relapse. After muscle relaxation (see Chapter 10), the client is asked to imagine a situation in which a lapse has occurred and, instead of continuing to drink, he or she successfully applies the emergency procedures. A detailed script should be negotiated with the client and then read aloud so that he or she can imagine the situation. An example of a relapse rehearsal script is as follows:

It is Friday evening and you are in Asquith's bar with Kevin and Barry. You are standing at the bar drinking a beer. Imagine yourself leaning against the bar holding your glass. Hear the sounds in the bar—the chatter of voices; glasses clinking; music in the background.

You have set a limit of three beers tonight and you are now on your third. You are trying to make it last until closing time and you are doing fine. Then the conversation turns into an argument about girls. Barry says that he doesn't like your current girlfriend. He says "I don't know what you see in her. She's boring and she's only going out with you because you've got a car." You feel angry. You think what he is saying is untrue.

As you argue, you notice that you have finished your drink faster than you meant to. Kevin buys you another drink and sets it on the counter. Barry says, "I think she's two-timing you anyway. I saw her speaking to Gerry last week." You lift the beer and take a long drink.

At this point, you realise that you are getting so angry with Barry that you feel like hitting him, and also that you have gone over your drinking limit. You stop drinking. You are pleased that you have recognised the high-risk situation.

You say to yourself, "I decided to cut down my drinking to avoid fights. If I stay here and drink, I'll end up hitting Barry. Barry is being a real pain and I can't stop him—that's just how he is. I am going to leave the bar. I will leave right now, without drinking the rest of my beer. Kevin may think it's odd, and Barry may think he's won, but who cares? I'll be the winner in the long run."

You feel calm and in control. You say to your friends, "I'm leaving. I'll give you a ring during the week to see if you fancy going to the match next weekend. See you soon."

You leave before they have time to persuade you to stay. Outside in the street you feel good. You have avoided getting drunk, and you have avoided a fight. You are impressed with your ability to control events. You smile to yourself as you walk home.

Graded Practice

So far, skills training for coping with temptation and coping with lapses has not required the client actually to encounter real-life high-risk situations. The methods described so far are all cognitive interventions—positive self-statements, decision review, distraction, covert modelling, cognitive reframing, formulating emergency procedures, and relapse rehearsal. These cognitive strategies may be viewed as useful preparation for real-life practice. Up to now, the client may have been asked to avoid high-risk situations until coping skills have been taught: avoidance is an option identified by adolescents as useful for controlling drinking (Brown & Stetson, 1988). However, since high-risk situations cannot be avoided for ever, it is essential eventually to practise these coping skills in real-life. Of course, some offenders may not be in the position to do this because they are in prison or otherwise unable to practise coping skills *in situ*, in which case a graded practice plan should be designed for use when the client returns to his or her own environment.

In the assessment, a hierarchy of high-risk situations should have been listed for each client. In graded practice, the client should be set homework assignments where there is planned exposure to a series of progressively more risky drinking situations in which he or she can apply coping skills. Annis (1990) suggests that assignments should be designed so that the client interprets the experience as: (1) *challenging*, that is, the situation is one which in the past would usually have resulted in heavy drinking; (2) *non-aversive*, that is, requiring only a moderate degree of effort in controlling drinking; (3) *unaided*, that is, success is not attributed to help from others; (4) *self-controlled*, that is, success is attributed to personal skills;

(5) *relevant*, that is, the situation in which control was exercised is seen as relevant to the drinking problem; (6) *general*, that is, the success is seen as part of an overall pattern of improvement. These six inferences should have a positive effect on self-efficacy judgments by the client.

In setting homework assignments, the following procedures should be followed:

1. Start with the easiest situation. The aim is to encourage the development of self-efficacy, and this can be done only by allowing the client to experience mastery over a situation, particularly in the early stages of graded practice.
2. Discuss the situation with the client in advance to identify any likely difficulties and to generate a number of possible coping strategies to deal with these.
3. Rehearse these coping strategies in role-play.
4. Discuss emergency procedures to employ should a lapse occur.
5. After the assignment has been undertaken, review the behaviour, reinforcing the use of coping strategies and examining difficulties.

Marlatt (1985a) recommends that relapse prevention should also include global coping strategies, such as problem solving and correcting lifestyle imbalance, so that the client can establish a broader framework for the prevention of relapse rather than coping with one high-risk situation after another. These global strategies will be addressed in the next chapter.

Summary

Relapse prevention is based on the identification of those situations in which the client is at high risk of relapse into heavy drinking, and teaching the skills and strategies necessary for coping with these high-risk situations.

The components of relapse prevention are as follows:

1. Explanation of the coping versus cure rationale;
2. Assessment of high-risk situations;
3. Assessment of coping skills and self-efficacy;
4. Teaching methods of coping with temptation;
5. Cue exposure;
6. Covert modelling;
7. Teaching methods of coping with lapses;
8. Graded practice.

Chapter 10

Lifestyle Modification

Maintenance of change in the long term depends upon an overall alteration of lifestyle which will increase the person's resilience for coping with life's problems and stresses without using alcohol to excess. Attempts to reduce drinking and offending require that the person drinks less often, forsakes usual drinking venues which are trouble spots, and avoids drinking with friends who are likely to offend. Upon making these changes, a number of seemingly intractable problems may be uncovered, for example, boredom, loneliness, anxiety, or depression. Learning to solve life's problems effectively, to develop activities which are not related to drinking or offending, and to socialise with more pro-social peers are necessary for long-term maintenance of change. The main interventions of lifestyle modification are problem solving, relaxation training, and work and leisure counselling. Before going on to describe these more fully, evidence of the need for lifestyle modification will be given.

Spontaneous Remission

In the field of addictions, it has been observed that large numbers of people successfully change their behaviour without receiving any professional help. Spontaneous remission from the problematic use of substances has been the focus of recent research, since the identification of factors involved in the natural course of change may provide information which could be useful in developing effective interventions.

Tuchfeld (1981) studied 51 adult men and women who reported having had alcohol problems which they resolved without recourse to formal intervention, 40 becoming abstinent and 11 drinking occasionally. Reasons for change were personal illness or accident; extraordinary events (for example, humiliation, suicide attempts); religious conversion or experience; financial problems; direct intervention by family or friends; alcohol-related death or illness of another person; education about alcoholism; and legal problems. Initial resolutions to change required subsequent social and economic support, and change towards non-alcohol-related leisure pursuits. Stall (1983) studied 13 media-recruited ex-drinkers and also identified the importance of social support and development of non-drinking lifestyles in maintaining change.

In a study of 51 male young offenders who had reduced their alcohol consumption without formal intervention, McMurran and Whitman (1990) noted that social change was important in maintaining controlled drinking and young offenders frequently reported using strategies such as finding alternative activities, avoiding heavy-drinking friends, and avoiding situations where heavy drinking typically occurs. These young offenders also used limit setting and rate control strategies, but it seemed that they had moved on from these to introduce more global lifestyle changes in their attempts to manage their new reduced-drinking status.

Stall and Biernacki (1986) have suggested the following three-stage model of remission from problematic substance use:

Stage 1 The increase in negative consequences of substance use results in motivation to change.

Stage 2 A decision to change is made and action is taken.

Stage 3 Remitters attempt to manage their new identities and develop new reduced-drinking lifestyles.

Stall and Biernacki's (1986) model of spontaneous remission has obvious similarities with Prochaska and DiClemente's (1986) model of stages of change in psychotherapy (see Chapter 3). It is apparent from both models that whilst motivational techniques, behavioural self-control training, skills training, and relapse prevention all have importance in interventions to reduce alcohol consumption, more global lifestyle changes will also have to be addressed. These may be seen as preparation for maintaining positive change independently of the professional.

Assessment

The specific techniques presented in this chapter may be seen as directed at improving the client's overall satisfaction with life.

Table 10.1 Life satisfaction scale (after Sisson & Azrin, 1989)

This scale is designed to measure your current levels of satisfaction in 10 key areas of your life. Please circle the number which indicates how you feel today about each area.

	Completely satisfied	Completely unsatisfied
1. Drinking		1..2..3..4..5..6..7..8..9..10
2. Education/work		1..2..3..4..5..6..7..8..9..10
3. Money		1..2..3..4..5..6..7..8..9..10
4. Control over offending		1..2..3..4..5..6..7..8..9..10
5. Health/fitness		1..2..3..4..5..6..7..8..9..10
6. Leisure activities		1..2..3..4..5..6..7..8..9..10
7. Friendships		1..2..3..4..5..6..7..8..9..10
8. Close relationships		1..2..3..4..5..6..7..8..9..10
9. Problem solving		1..2..3..4..5..6..7..8..9..10
10. General happiness with life		1..2..3..4..5..6..7..8..9..10

Change may be monitored as the intervention progresses using a self-rating scale to determine the client's expressed satisfaction in 10 key areas. A life satisfaction scale adapted from Sisson and Azrin (1989) is presented in Table 10.1.

PROBLEM SOLVING

Problem solving training derives from the work of D'Zurilla and Gold-fried (1971) who viewed problem behaviours (which would include heavy drinking and crime) as ineffective means of coping with problematic situations. They define problem solving as a process which "(a) makes available a variety of potentially effective response alternatives for dealing with the problematic situation and (b) increases the probability of selecting the most effective response from among these various alternatives" (p. 108).

Effective problem solving may be described in five stages:

Orientation

D'Zurilla and Nezu (1982) describe the first stage as adopting a "problem-solving set" which consists of four important components: (a) the recognition of a problematic situation when one occurs; (b) the acceptance of the view that problematic situations are a normal part of life; (c) the expectation that one is capable of solving problems effectively;

and (d) the ability to stop and think instead of responding impulsively when confronted with a problematic situation.

One of the important identifying features of a problematic situation is a 'bad feeling'. This deliberately vague term allows the inclusion of a whole range of negative cognitive, emotional, and physical states— depression, anger, anxiety, boredom, withdrawal, craving, and so on. These bad feelings are not in themselves the problem, but should be used as cues for attending to and recognising the problematic situation which may be creating them. It is at this stage that successful problem solvers stop and think, whereas less successful problem solvers react impulsively and give up quickly if a solution is not immediately apparent.

Problem Definition and Goal Setting

The second step in effective problem solving is to define the problem clearly. This is often quite difficult since real-life problems are frequently complex and the facts of the situation may be distorted by the individual's beliefs, values, and assumptions. It is essential, however, that the problem is well defined so that relevant solutions may be generated.

D'Zurilla and Nezu (1982) suggest the following four components: (a) seek all available facts and information about the problem and describe these in clear, specific, concrete terms; (b) differentiate facts from inferences, and relevant from irrelevant facts; (c) identify the factors that are making the situation problematic; and (d) set realistic problem-solving goals.

Generation of Alternatives

The third stage is to generate strategies for attaining the goals. "Brainstorming" is a method whereby a person is encouraged to produce as many alternatives as possible (Osborn, 1963). Creativity is encouraged by deferment of judgment in that responses should not be censored at this stage, and emphasis on quantity, since the more ideas a person has overall, the greater will be the likelihood that some of these will be good ideas.

Decision Making and Action

After brainstorming a wide range of strategies, these should then be screened to eliminate the obviously impossible, impractical, and inadvisable. The remaining strategies should then be examined in terms of their advantages and disadvantages. It is important to note at this stage that no single strategy will offer a perfect solution to a problem: if the perfect solution did exist, it is unlikely that there would be a problem in the first place. After analysis of each strategy, the best options should be selected to form an action plan which should then be implemented in addressing the real-life problem situation.

Evaluation

After execution of the action plan, the problem solver should compare the observed outcome with the original goals. If the goals have been achieved satisfactorily, then the problem solving process can be terminated. If the goals have not been achieved, then the problem solving process may be repeated. Actual performance is likely to be affected by factors such as skill deficits or emotional inhibitions which may come to light during the action stage. It may help to divide each strategy into a number of smaller, less daunting steps, or the deficits and inhibitions may themselves be treated as primary problems and subjected to the problem solving process.

Chaney, O'Leary and Marlatt (1978) compared problem solving training with a placebo control (discussion groups) and a no-intervention control with men in an inpatient alcoholism treatment programme. At one-year follow-up, the problem solving group was compared with the two control groups combined and found to be significantly more improved on measures of number of days drunk, total number of drinks, and mean length of drinking periods. Although no significant difference was found in the number of relapses between groups, the duration and severity of relapses were reduced in those who received problem solving training.

Problem solving training has been used with imprisoned offenders as part of a cognitive skills training programme (Ross, Fabiano & Ross, 1986). Based on research evidence that offenders tend to be non-reflective and impulsive and therefore react to problematic situations without first stopping to think, specific skills are taught to enable the offender to recognise, analyse, and solve problematic situations. Comparisons of programme participants with a no-intervention control group showed significantly greater pre- to post-intervention improvements on an impulsivity scale for those in the treatment group, and at follow-up around 18 months after release from prison, offenders in the treatment group had been readmitted to prison with new convictions at a lower rate than the control group (Robinson, Grossman & Porporino, 1991).

In practice, problem solving may be introduced by teaching the

Table 10.2   Problem solving pro forma

1. Bad Feelings?
   Boredom

2. What is my problem?
   It's Saturday afternoon and I've got nothing to do today or this evening

3. What are my goals?
   (a) *Find some activity that will be interesting*
   (b) *Avoid getting drunk*

4. What are my options?	Pros	Cons
(a) *Go to the cinema*	*There's a good film on.*	*It costs a lot. I've no one to go with.*
(b) *Watch television*	*It would fill in the afternoon.*	*There's nothing I want to watch.*
(c) *Buy some cans of beer and get drunk*	*It would make the television seem more interesting.*	*It's too early to start drinking.*
(d) *Go swimming*	*I need to keep fit.*	*It's too cold. It's boring.*
(e) *Visit my brother*	*I'd like to see my niece.*	*He may not be in. He may be busy.*
(f) *Go to the pub at night*	*My mates might be there. It would be fun.*	*I might get drunk. I might get into trouble.*

5. What is my plan?
   (a) *Phone my brother to see if I can visit.*
   (b) *Go to the cinema.*
   (c) *Go to the pub later on in the evening so that I don't drink too much.*

6. How did I do?
   I went to my brother's house and played with my niece for a while. Then I went to the cinema. It didn't cost as much as drinking would have and I enjoyed the film. I still had time to go to the pub and meet my friends. I had a couple of drinks but didn't get drunk or get into trouble.

offender to ask the following six questions in sequence: (1) Bad feelings? (2) What is my problem? (3) What are my goals? (4) What are my options? (5) What is my plan? (6) How did I do? This may be presented as a written exercise and a pro forma with a simple worked example is given in Table 10.2.

TRAINING IN RELAXATION

It is widely believed that one of the effects of alcohol is to reduce stress, anxiety, or tension. Reviews of research on this function of alcohol reveal a complex picture which shows that that alcohol does reduce stress in some people under certain conditions (Young, Oei & Knight, 1990; Wilson, 1988). The power of alcohol to reduce stress depends upon variables such as the quantity consumed, the effects expected by the drinker, and the setting in which drinking occurs. In clinical populations, anxiety disorders such as agoraphobia and social phobia have been seen to precede the onset of heavy drinking, with alcohol being used as a form of self-medication. Adolescent alcohol abusers have been reported as experiencing a higher incidence of stressful life events than non-abusers, although it is not clear if life events trigger alcohol abuse or vice versa (Brown, 1989). Stress not only triggers problem drinking in some people but also precipitates relapse in those who are trying to control their drinking; negative emotional states, interpersonal conflict, and social pressure account for most relapses (Marlatt, 1985b; see Chapter 9).

Stressors are environmental or psychological events which challenge the individual. Stressors have been classified into three categories: (1) cataclysmic events, such as natural disaster or war, which have a sudden, powerful, and widespread impact; (2) personal stressors, such as death of a loved one or losing one's job, which are again powerful but affect fewer people; and (3) chronic background stressors or "daily hassles", such as job dissatisfaction, relationship problems, or lack of money, which are stable, repetitive, low intensity problems (Lazarus & Cohen, 1977). The degree to which any potential stressor will actually produce a stress response in the individual depends upon a number of factors: how a person appraises the situation, the skills a person has for coping with stressors, and the amount of social support available.

When a stressor is appraised in a negative light and the person does not have adequate coping skills or social support to deal with the situation, a stress response may occur. The stress response has physical, cognitive, emotional, and behavioural components. An acute stress response is typified by increased muscle tension, increased heart rate, sweating, inability to concentrate, feelings of anxiety, and "nervous energy". If the stress is prolonged, there may be a change to fatigue, depression, and physical ill-health.

Relaxation training as a method of coping with stress derives from the work of Jacobson (1929), who devised a system of progressive muscle relaxation based on the premise that muscle tension is closely related to anxiety and that the experience of anxiety will be reduced if tense muscles can be made to relax. Over the years, relaxation training has developed to include cognitive components based on the fundamentals of meditation. There is evidence to show that relaxation training reduces alcohol consumption in drinkers who show high pre-treatment levels of anxiety. Rosenberg (1979, cited in Miller & Hester, 1986a) compared relaxation training and alcohol education in alcoholics and found that relaxation training produced significantly greater reductions in alcohol consumption in those clients who scored high on an anxiety scale. Similarly, Rohsenow, Smith and Johnson (1986) found that a stress management intervention with college students reduced alcohol consumption at six-month follow-up, with the most anxious and heaviest drinkers showing the greatest change.

Relaxation techniques which may be used in intervention are: (1) identification of activities which the client personally finds relaxing; (2) progressive muscle relaxation; and (3) imagery exercises.

Relaxing Activities

Each of us has his or her own preferred activities for coping with stress. Brainstorming with the client will identify a variety of such activities, which may include:

- going for a walk
- listening to music
- reading a book
- watching television
- taking a bath
- talking to a friend
- taking physical exercise, such as jogging or swimming

Muscle Relaxation

There are several different muscle relaxation programmes. The following set of instructions provides one example. First, ensure that the client is sitting comfortably, then say the instructions slowly in a calm, gentle voice. Each stretching exercise should be presented twice in succession before moving on to the next.

Relaxation Instructions

I am going to ask you to tense and relax muscle groups in all parts of your body, one after the other. Tension is simply flexing and stretching: you should not clench your muscles tight. Please concentrate on the difference between tension and relaxation.

First, stretch your legs and point your toes ... and hold that position for a few seconds ... now relax.

— Now press your knees together ... hold ... and relax.
— Pull in your stomach ... hold ... and relax.
— Arch your lower back ... hold ... and relax.
— Tighten your upper back and chest muscles ... hold ... and relax.
— Press your elbows to your sides ... hold ... and relax.
— Stretch out your arms and spread out your fingers ... hold ... and relax.
— Shrug your shoulders ... hold ... and relax.
— Stretch your neck by turning your head first one way ... then the other ... and relax.
— Raise your eyebrows ... hold ... and relax.
— Now scowl ... hold ... and relax.

I want you now to attend to each part of your body in turn to make sure that there is no tension. Your feet are relaxed ... your calf muscles are relaxed ... and your thighs are relaxed. There is no tension in your stomach ... or your back ... or your chest. Your hands are relaxed ... and your arms are relaxed. Let your shoulders drop ... and remove all tension from your face.

Now sit for a few moments, close your eyes, and concentrate on your breathing. Each time you breathe out, say to yourself the word "relax" ... "relax"...

When you feel ready, open your eyes, stretch as you would when waking in the morning, and continue with your usual activities feeling calm and relaxed.

The purpose of using the word "relax" in the final stage is to build up an association between the word itself and the relaxed state so that eventually simply saying the word "relax" to oneself will go some way to inducing the relaxed state. This is obviously useful in stressful situations where it is not possible to carry out the full relaxation procedure.

Imagery

Muscle relaxation may be augmented by imagery techniques, that is the visualisation of calming objects or scenes. The client may be able to concentrate upon a flickering candle, a glass of carbonated water with bubbles gently rising to the surface, or white clouds drifting across a blue sky. Alternatively, a guided imagery scene may be presented to the client. This should be agreed in advance between the counsellor and client to determine personal preferences. Having a client imagine floating in a warm sea, for example, may not be particularly relaxing for a person who cannot swim.

One commonly used guided imagery scene is as follows:

> Imagine yourself on a deserted beach. The sun is shining from a clear blue sky. Feel the warmth of the sun on your skin. You are lying on the sand and it feels soft and comfortable. You hear the sound of the waves on the shore. They rush in as you breathe in, and ebb as you breathe out. In ... and out. In ... and out. Each time the waves ebb, you feel your tension being carried away on the water. Continue to imagine this scene ... the warmth of the sun on your skin ... the softness of the sand ... the waves carrying your tension away ... until you feel completely relaxed.

The effectiveness of muscle relaxation and imagery can be measured using a subjective rating scale on which clients may estimate their levels of tension—relaxation before and after relaxation practice. A rating scale adapted from Monti, Abrams, Kadden and Cooney (1989) is presented in Table 10.3. Relaxation, like most other skills, requires practice and the client should be instructed to spend at least 10 minutes each day using this technique. Clients should be advised not to expect immediate benefits but a reduction in tension or anxiety will be effected gradually by regular practice.

Table 10.3 Tension—relaxation rating scale (after Monti, Abrams, Kadden & Cooney, 1989)

Estimate and record your present degree of tension—relaxation using the following scale. Your rating may be any number from 1—100.

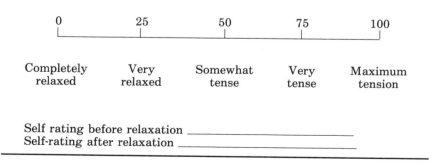

Self rating before relaxation _____
Self-rating after relaxation _____

WORK AND LEISURE LIFESTYLE CHANGES

Maintenance of a reduced drinking lifestyle depends upon the degree to which it is socially reinforced and the client should therefore be advised to rearrange his or her social environment appropriately. The key areas which will be addressed in this section are work and leisure activities. If employment and leisure activities can be organised so that the individual is engaging in pro-social activities with pro-social peers, then the likelihood of heavy drinking and offending will be reduced.

In young adults, the transition into adult work and family roles in their late 20s is associated with a decrease in alcohol use and delinquency (Temple & Ladouceur, 1986). Gender difference is apparent, however, in that work status is a more significant predictor of alcohol use in young men, whereas family status is a more significant predictor of alcohol use in young women (Frank, Jacobson and Tuer, 1990).

Sisson and Azrin (1989) describe the Community Reinforcement Approach (CRA) to encouraging abstinence in alcoholics. This intervention combines Antabuse treatment, marriage counselling, employment counselling, social skills training, recreational advice, and relaxation training. CRA compared favourably with a standard hospital treatment programme in that CRA-treated patients drank on fewer days and were employed on more days. Social and job-finding skills were seen to be most useful with single people, whose social support depends upon relationships other than that of a spouse or partner.

Work

Employment counselling may be seen as a specialist aspect of intervention. Offenders may be directed to their local JobCentre, where they will be given information about Job Club and Restart schemes. Specialist advice is available from NACRO (see List of Resources Section). Many professionals will, however, wish to address issues of employment with their clients and procedures for doing this will be described.

Assets

The first step is to identify the client's assets by identifying experience and skills in a number of different areas, as presented in Table 10.4. Specific activities in each area should be listed on the table,

Table 10.4 Employment assets

Type of activity	Specific activities	Skills required
Best subjects at school		
Qualifications		
Work experience		
Voluntary work		
Interest/hobbies		

along with the skills required for that activity. For example, within the category of work experience, delivering newspapers would be a specific activity and the skills required would be the ability to rise early in the morning, good timekeeping, and being able to organise oneself to deliver the right paper to the right house. Skills relevant to other types of activity might include numeracy, literacy, physical strength and fitness, the ability to get on with people, and good personal appearance. Identifying assets helps an offender to realise what he or she might have to offer a potential employer.

Job Selection

The next stage is to identify what job-type might suit each offender by listing the most important features he or she is looking for in a job. These might include good pay, working out of doors, working with people, having weekends off, being near home, and so on. A variety of possible jobs can then be listed under appropriate headings, for example:

1. *Working with people*: shop assistant; waiter/waitress; hospital porter; receptionist; hairdresser.
2. *Working out of doors*: farm hand; gardener; postman/woman; builder's labourer; window cleaner.
3. *Office work*: secretary; clerk: telephonist.
4. *Practical work*: cleaner; packer; stores assistant; factory worker; driver's mate.
5. *Skilled trades*: bricklayer; plumber; electrician; mechanic; carpenter; painter and decorator.

Assets and preferences should be matched with specific jobs which may then be targeted in a job search.

Job Search

Advice about the places to look for jobs will be useful to the client. These include: JobCentres, newspaper advertisements, vacancy boards in shop windows or outside factories, asking friends and relatives if they know of vacancies, and contacting local businesses by letter or telephone to enquire about vacancies. It should be stressed that these sources of information should be checked regularly and several job applications may be made simultaneously: a job will almost certainly not be found immediately.

Making Contact

First contact with potential employers will be made in a variety of ways, each of which should be practised in role play or written exercises using sample job advertisements. Specific skills which need to be addressed are:

1. making telephone calls to ask for an application form or request an interview;
2. writing letters to ask for an application form or offer services;
3. completing application forms;
4. visiting worksites to enquire about vacancies.

Interviews

Clients should be advised to prepare for interviews by finding out about the firm and the job, considering what they have to offer the employer, and attending to practicalities such as travelling arrangements and dress. Interview skills may then be practised in role-play.

The issue of admitting to a criminal record should be addressed in employment counselling. It is not necessary to volunteer this information, but it is neither wise nor lawful to lie if asked direct questions about convictions.

Ashmore and Jarvie (1987) describe employment counselling with imprisoned young offenders which included identifying assets, advice about job search strategies, role-playing telephone calls and interviews, and skills training for getting on with work colleagues. Course participants showed improvement in three areas: (1) knowledge about job finding; (2) self-presentation over the telephone; and (3) interview skills. At follow-up 4—12 weeks after release, those who undertook the programme showed evidence of having made more effort to find a job in comparison with a no-intervention control. Hall, Loeb, Coyne and Cooper (1981) describe a behaviourally-based job seekers' workshop for heroin users on probation or parole. Their 11-hour programme included instructions in completing application forms, job search procedures, and role-playing interviews. Those who completed the programme were compared with a group who received a three-hour information workshop, and showed greater improvements in interview skills and at 12-week follow-up 86% of the experimental group had found employment as compared with 54% of the information-only control group.

Leisure Activities

Being realistic, it must be recognised that many offenders will take some time to find employment and a few may never achieve this goal. It is important, therefore, to address use of leisure time so that this may be used as constructively as possible. Analysis of leisure time has shown that teenage offenders spend more time away from their homes engaged in unstructured street activities with their friends than do non-offenders (Riley, 1987). This type of lifestyle presents the young person with opportunities for offending and, because of this, changes are warranted. Leisure counselling procedures are outlined by McGuire and Priestley (1985) and include the following components:

Activity Diaries

Individuals can assess how they spend their time by completing an activity diary retrospectively for a specific recent week or a "typical" week, or concurrently over a period of one or two weeks. A daily timetable may be used to chart how specific time periods during mornings, afternoons, evenings, and nights are spent. Each activity should be rated on a satisfaction scale to help identify preferences, and note should be taken of whether or not drinking was part of the activity. A daily timetable pro forma is presented in Table 10.5.

Diaries may be analysed to assess the percentage time spent in different types of activities, such as survival activities (for example, shopping, cleaning, and cooking), various leisure pursuits, and unstructured activities (such as "hanging out" with friends). The overall satisfaction rating for each activity should be calculated, along with the incidence of drinking in each type of situation.

Table 10.5 Daily activity diary

Day _____

	Time	Activity	Satisfaction (Rate on a scale of 1–10, where 1 = very boring and 10 = very satisfying)	Drinking 0 = None 1 = Light 2 = Moderate 3 = Heavy 4 = Very heavy
Morning				
Afternoon				
Evening				
Night				

Brainstorming

A list of possible activities may be generated by brainstorming, a technique described earlier in the chapter. The aim at this stage is to produce a quantity of ideas, leaving decisions about the practicalities until later.

Surveys

Clients may be set the task of gathering information about local leisure facilities and events from libraries, information offices, and newspapers. Where possible, they may undertake projects to find out detailed information, such as leisure centre opening hours and membership fees, or the programme and meeting times of a club or society. If offenders cannot go out to seek this information, speakers could be invited to visit an institution to discuss recreational pursuits.

Planning Ahead

Using a timetable similar to that presented in Table 10.5, the client can be asked to plan daily activities in advance. The information gathered in the preceding stages should be used in emphasising preferred activities which are not related to drinking and introducing new leisure pursuits. It is worth alerting the client to the fact that it may take time to benefit from new activities, since initially there may be discomfort created by feeling inexpert, unfit, or not knowing people.

It helps to have a friend along to lend moral support and, with persistence, the difficulties recede. Indeed, in time, new activities may become "positive addictions" (Glasser, 1976).

It is worth pointing out here the specific importance of health-related behaviours, which may be included in an activity programme. In a study of 1588 American adolescents, Donovan, Jessor and Costa (1991) observed a negative relationship between problem behaviours and health-related behaviours: greater degrees of involvement in problem behaviours were seen to be related to less involvement in health-related behaviours. Problem behaviours included delinquency, problem drinking, cigarette smoking, and illicit drug use; positive health-related behaviours included regular exercise, healthy eating, and adequate sleeping. Even at the stage of identifying problem behaviours and health-related behaviours an overlap between the two areas becomes apparent: drinking, smoking, and drug use may be classified "problem behaviours" because they are socially sanctioned in young people, but they are clearly also health-compromising behaviours. Donovan, Jessor and Costa (1991) suggest that attempts to change any part of this problem behaviour pattern may need to deal with the pattern as a whole, which would include increasing health-related behaviours.

Marlatt (1985d) points out the importance of attending to exercise and diet in lifestyle-modification interventions. Protracted heavy drinking may have taken its toll on a person's physical condition and improved diet and exercise will help redress the balance. In addition, physical health and fitness will increase resilience for coping with stress. Apart from the direct beneficial effects of a healthy lifestyle, health-related behaviours may be seen as inconsistent with health-compromising behaviours, with cognitive dissonance created where there is engagement in both. This dissonance may be reduced through a reduction in drinking, smoking, and drug use. Health-related behaviours, such as participating in sporting activities, eating regular meals, and having sensible sleeping patterns should, therefore, be programmed into an activities schedule.

Summary

Maintenance of change in the long-term depends upon an overall alteration of lifestyle whereby the client learns to solve life's problems effectively without using alcohol to excess, develop activities which are not related to drinking and offending, and associate with more pro-social peers. The main areas to address in a lifestyle modification intervention are:

- Problem solving
- Relaxation
- Work
- Leisure activities

Chapter 11

Evaluation

From time to time we are both involved in the training of practitioners who work with offenders, and on many occasions during such work we have observed something rather curious. When we talk about assessment and practice this generates a great deal of interest; when we talk about theories this can also excite debate; when we talk about the development of policies and strategies to maximise the impact of working with offenders everybody has an opinion. But when we talk about evaluation most practitioners glaze over or gently nod off to sleep. Why does the topic of evaluation have this effect?

When talking about evaluation to practitioners one meets two main types of argument as to why evaluation is not routinely carried out. The first point of opposition is that evaluation is a luxury, something for which there is simply no time. In the busy life of the practitioner there is no space for evaluation of practice (anyway, the argument goes, it is best not to look too closely at what you are doing or you might be in for a shock). The second line of opposition is that the process of evaluation is too complex. Practitioners are trained to practise; pursuits such as evaluation are best left to researchers and academics who have the resources for such things.

We disagree with both arguments. Evaluation is not a luxury or optional extra, it is *the* crucial component in good professional practice. Evaluation does not have to be complex, anyone can very quickly master the basics of sound evaluation. To support our position, in this chapter we will present our arguments for evaluation and describe the principles of evaluation.

WHY CONDUCT EVALUATIONS?

Good Practice

There are two strong practical reasons to encourage evaluation of intervention programmes. The first is that many intervention programmes last for a lengthy period, weeks or even months, and even though the intervention is successful the rate of change can be slow. This process of slow, often imperceptible, change can have three effects: the practitioner fails to perceive change; the client fails to perceive change; both the client and practitioner fail to perceive change. However, a record of change over time can be used to challenge perceptions of limited progress. Provided some basic rules are adhered to (see below), a concrete record of change can serve to reinforce both the practitioner and the client in maintaining their working relationship. In particular, a record of progress can help greatly in those situations where the client wants to drop out of a programme because they feel it is not working.

The second practical reason for carrying out evaluations is that if an intervention is not working, then the practitioner will be able to detect this at an early stage and take the appropriate corrective action. Once any "fine tuning" has taken place, consistent evaluation will allow the effects of the changes to be detected.

In truth, both these practical reasons are different sides of the same coin: systematically looking to see whether what we are doing has any effect; and seeing whether the intervention has the planned effect. We often start with the assumption that our programmes will be beneficial to our clients. However, our interventions are not guaranteed to be beneficial and it is surely good professional practice to check whether we are working to good effect, to no effect, or even to the detriment of those with whom we work.

Improving Practice

Another function of evaluation is that it allows us to begin to improve the quality of our practice. A recent study that one of us was involved in provides a perfect example of this function of evaluation (Savage, Hollin & Hayward, 1990). This study was concerned with the effects of a self-help manual for problems drinkers issued to individuals who felt they had a drink problem but did not want help through a formal agency. Given that the intervention was to be conducted by post and by telephone, we were interested in two questions: are self-help manuals effective when used in this way?; and what component of self-help manuals contributes most to their effects (if any)?

In the first stage of the study the volunteers completed a set of assessment measures to provide information on severity of alcohol dependence and level of alcohol consumption. When the assessment was complete, the self-help materials were dispatched by post. Now, self-help manuals for problem drinkers typically contain two types of material: these are educational information about alcohol and its effects, and guidelines for self-management of one's own drinking. It was the relative effectiveness of these two components that was of interest, alongside whether the complete package had any effect on alcohol consumption. In the next phase of the study one group of volunteers received a package of educational self-help material, while the other group received a package of self-management self-help material. Over the period of assimilating this information the volunteers continued to monitor their drinking using a standard protocol. In the final phase of the study, after reporting their drinking back to us, there was a cross-over of material: the group that had received the educational package now received the self-help material and *vice versa*. Again using the same protocol, the volunteers continued to monitor their drinking during this second phase of the study.

Thus, in summary, we had delivered the same package of material to all the volunteers, so that there was no ethical problem regarding withholding treatment. We had, however, reversed the order of delivery of the components of the manual. This design would therefore allow us to make some comments about the general effectiveness of our self-help package, and the contribution to effectiveness, if any, of the educational and self-help components.

The results indicated that both groups showed a significant reduction in alcohol consumption over the time spanned by the study. The average levels of consumption fell from an average across all the volunteers of about 59 standard units before treatment, to 34 units after the intervention. (Our unpublished follow-up data show that these positive changes were maintained nine months after the end of the formal delivery of the programme.) However, there was an effect associated with order of presentation. The group that received the self-help material first showed an immediate and marked reduction in their drinking; the following educational material then further lowered the level of drinking. The group that received the educational material first showed a very different pattern of change. When initially using the educational material their drinking remained virtually unchanged, and it was only when the self-help material was delivered that their drinking began to improve noticeably.

The results of this study are informative in two ways. Firstly, they inform us that, overall, our service delivery is effective: the self-help programme is effective in doing what it is supposed to do—cut down drinking. Secondly, the results tell us that the order of components is important: essentially, when people ask for help they do not need telling how awful the effects of drink can be, they need strategies to begin to deal with what they have acknowledged to be a problem. Later, once behaviour is beginning to change, then the educational material might be important in reinforcing the changes. While our study does not say that educational material is redundant—a different research design would be required to test this hypothesis—it does suggest that educational material should be presented after the self-management material for people in the action stage of change. Clearly this is a point that we should be aware of for our future practice. Indeed, if only a brief intervention is possible, then clearly self-management strategies are to be preferred to educational measures.

In summary, the Savage *et al.* (1990) study provides an example of evaluation that is useful and informative but did not demand huge investments of time and resources. Two of those involved were practitioners carrying out work they would have been involved in anyway, while the other was able to provide a little help with design, analysis, and publication. We simply attended to the essential ingredients for evaluation as noted below.

THE ESSENTIALS OF EVALUATION

The key to good evaluation lies in planning or designing the evaluation before starting the programme. This involves deciding on the type of design, deciding on suitable evaluative measures, and settling on the appropriate mode of analysis. There are several helpful guides to setting up research projects such as that written by Herbert (1990) and McMurran and Baldwin (1990).

Design

There are two basic types of design used in outcome evaluation research: these are group designs and single-case designs.

Group Designs

Group designs are probably the most frequently used types of design in outcome evaluation. Typically they involve delivery of the intervention to a group of individuals who form the *treatment group*. Using some measure of performance or outcome, typically given before and after the intervention, the progress of the treatment group is then compared with another group, the *control group*, who do not participate in treatment. In this type of design a control group is necessary to establish that it is the intervention that has been instrumental in bringing about any change. Thus, in the study discussed above, the criticism could rightly be levelled that while the general effect of the self-help manual was positive, how could we know that it was the intervention that brought about the reduction in drinking? It could be that we had a group that were about to change anyway and that their drinking would have lessened regardless of any intervention. The response to this view is that previous studies have demonstrated the effectiveness of self-help manuals and we therefore had no need to rediscover the wheel. The original research on the self-help materials would have used control groups to show the efficacy of the self-help material; most probably using random allocation of problem drinkers to treatment and control groups to minimise the risk of a selection effect.

While group designs are, of course, informative about the effects of treatment they are not without their drawbacks. There are ethical objections to the use of a no-treatment control group, based on the view that it is not in the client's best interests either to be refused treatment, or to have treatment delayed in the case of a "waiting list control" design, or some spurious intervention as with "placebo attention" control groups. However, this view is problematic in that it supposes that to receive treatment is in the client's best interest. With new and untried techniques or treatment packages this might not be the case: to be in the no treatment control might well be the most healthy option.

A practical problem, encountered by anyone who has attempted this type of evaluative research, lies in *matching* the treatment and control groups. Clearly it is desirable that both groups resemble one another as closely as possible. There would be little merit, for example, in testing the outcome of a self-help manual using a treatment group of middle-aged physiologically-dependent drinkers, compared with a no-treatment control group of adolescent problem drinkers. With treatment and control groups it is desirable to compare like with like, and the researcher must decide which of the dimensions it is important to match (e.g. age; duration of drinking; level of dependence on alcohol). Having made this decision, the researcher is faced with the task of finding sufficient numbers of matched individuals to participate in the study. Needless to say, this often proves highly difficult, thereby demanding more and more complex statistical adjustments when analysing the data.

A much more serious problem, from a professional standpoint if not from a research perspective, lies in the data management techniques that are used with studies that employ group designs. Group designs are based on looking for differences *between* groups; they are informative about the average performance of one group compared to another group. However, concern with the average performance between groups can mask variations *within* groups. In the Savage *et al.* (1990) study noted above, for example, there was an average reduction in self-reported drinking for the whole study population (i.e. both groups). However, our "inside knowledge" of the individual variations in self-reported reductions in drinking revealed that some individuals reported a great deal of change, others only a modicum, while some others reported very little. Indeed, it is possible to have some individuals who actually do worse with treatment, but this is masked by aggregating their performance with that of others who improve.

Of course, researchers are aware of these effects and can attempt to control them statistically or through variations in sampling. This is well and good from a research perspective when a sensitive analysis of within-group variations can be informative; however, it is less than helpful from the point of view of a practitioner. We deliver interventions not to achieve a net mean improvement, but to try to help engineer an improvement for each and every client.

The conclusion to be drawn from this line of thought is that while group designs are important in treatment outcome research, they are of somewhat limited value to practitioners concerned with whether their client is showing change. To achieve this level of evaluation it is necessary to move away from group designs to single-case evaluations.

Single-case Designs

With single-case designs the emphasis shifts from the group to the individual as the unit of analysis. While there are many variations on the theme of single case design (Barlow & Hersen, 1984), the most frequently employed design uses the three stages of baseline, intervention, and return to baseline.

The *baseline* phase, usually referred to as the "A" phase, is the period during which assessment details are gathered from the individual client. Before commencing with baseline measurement, the decision must be made on what is to be measured. There are no strict rules about what can and can not be measured: it might be levels of self-reported drinking, blood alcohol levels, peer reports of drinking, and so on. The decision might be made to assess just one of these or some combination: when more than one assessment is taken this is called a *multiple baseline*. The important point to note is that, once selected, the assessment must remain constant over the evaluation. It is not satisfactory, for example, to switch from self-reported to peer reported drinking as a measure during the evaluation.

During the baseline period, as much information as possible should be gathered to give as accurate a picture as possible of the client's behaviour. Typically, this information is shown in graph form which can be highly revealing in itself. Suppose you are monitoring self-reported drinking with an individual client, and that the client produces a report of units drunk every day over a 14-day period. A variety of types of baseline could emerge from such an assessment. A *stable* baseline would show that the drinking remained constant over the baseline period; a *decreasing* baseline would suggest that the drinking is becoming less frequent (which might well be a reactive effect of the process of baseline recording); and an *increasing* baseline, like that in Figure 11.1, shows that the drinking is becoming more of a problem.

For the practitioner collecting baseline information, this process is valuable in forming a clear picture of what is happening with a given client. Changes over the baseline period may provide clues to what triggers, say, drinking binges; a multiple baseline might offer some clues as to the inter-relationship between, say, states of anxiety and drinking. To repeat an earlier point, a good baseline provides an accurate, agreed summary for both practitioner and client of the state of affairs before beginning the intervention.

The intervention phase, termed the "B" phase, is marked by the point at which the intervention begins. It does not matter what the intervention is from a design point of view: it can be behavioural self-control training, cue exposure, stress management, or whatever else is appropriate. Further, a single-case design does *not* mean that the intervention has to be on a one-to-one basis; the intervention can equally well take place in a group. The crucial point is that you monitor each individual's progress not the average of the group. As with baseline recording, repeated measures of performance are taken over the intervention period, using the same index of change. This continual monitoring will reveal whether or not the client responds to what is being offered. If there is improvement, this is obviously what is hoped for; if there is no change, then clearly some alternative approach needs to be considered. Without this careful monitoring of a defined and agreed index of change it is difficult during treatment to make judgments of this sort.

In the final stage there is what is usually called a "return to base-line", but is perhaps better thought of as a follow-up period after the completion of the formal stage of the intervention. The continued monitoring of performance during this second A-phase allows the practitioner to see whether any gains over the treatment phase have been maintained. If gains are maintained this is well and good; if not then further "booster" sessions are probably needed.

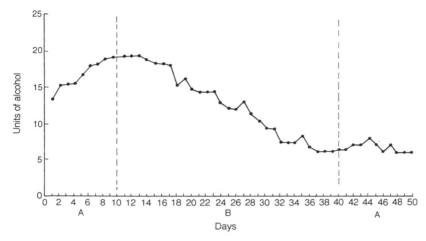

Figure 11.1 Single case evaluation using A-B-A design

The case illustrated below (summarised in Figure 11.1) provides an example of an A-B-A design applied to assess the effects of a controlled drinking programme.

Example of a single-case evaluation

The example given below provides an illustration of a single case approach to monitoring an individual's progress through assessment, intervention, and follow-up. In this instance the evaluation measure is self-reported units of alcohol, although any number of other outcome measures can be used as deemed appropriate. The essential point is that the same measure is used consistently throughout the evaluation. Indeed, you may elect to use more than one measure, say self-reported drinking together with an estimate of drinking by a family member. Clearly there are advantages to using multiple measures rather than relying solely on one measure.

In Figure 11.1, above, the first phase (labelled "A") is referred to as the baseline phase during which the individual monitors the amount he or she drinks. A drink diary is often provided to assist in self-recording. In the diagram the amount the individual reports drinking is increasing over the 10-day baseline period: while there may be several explanations for this rise, the self-report information provides a reasonable starting point for appreciating the scale of the problem drinking. During the intervention phase, labelled "B", the treatment procedures are brought into play. From the point of view of evaluation, it does not matter what procedures are used, only that the same procedure is used consistently throughout. [It is beyond the scope of this book to discuss multiple treatment evaluations, those interested should refer to Barlow and Hersen (1984).] In the example given here, the decision was made to end the formal intervention after a period of 30 days as the self-reported frequency of drinking had fallen considerably.

During the 10-day follow-up period, also labelled "A" to indicate a return to non-intervention conditions, the self-reported drinking stayed at a low level, indicating that the individual concerned was able to maintain the progress made over the intervention phase. At this point the practitioner has a number of choices to make—to discontinue client contact; to maintain contact, perhaps on a less frequent basis; or to move to some other area of work—that will depend on the individual circumstances of the client concerned.

Dissemination and Publication

As with evaluation generally, there is sometimes a general feeling expressed that publication is something that other people do— academics and others who have the time, training, and resources, but certainly not busy practitioners. We take the opposite view: to have carried out an evaluation that other practitioners would learn from, and then not to disseminate this knowledge, is less than desirable.

The process of dissemination of one's work can be both formal and informal. Regular "in-house" research seminars, at which colleagues present details of their work, can be enormously helpful to all concerned. Further, there are many conferences at which workshops and papers can be presented to a wider audience. Giving presentations at such conferences has the dual function of not only making your own work known, but can be the source of an exchange of information through meeting others working in the same area of work and tackling the same issues.

Just as speaking in public about one's work can take place on several levels, similarly publication can be at various levels. Rather like in-house seminars, many organisations have in-house newsletters or bulletins that can provide a perfect outlet for an account of evaluative work. Moving to wider readership there are a number of professional magazines, say for social workers, probation officers, nurses, or psychologists, that carry accounts of evaluative work. Finally, there are the many research journals that publish formal accounts of research: a list of some of the main ones is provided in the List of Resources Section.

Publishing in the academic journals is a little more demanding as there are generally some technical rules about submission of papers. These rules differ from journal to journal and before considering writing for a given journal it is essential to be familiar with that particular publication. It is important to read several issues of the journal to get a feel for the type of material the journal favours, and to read the specific instructions for submission of material. It would be false to say that writing for publication is easy: it demands time, patience and, above all, a knowledge of the rules of the publishing game. For these reasons we advise collaboration at the outset with an experienced writer for specialist publications. There are, of course, many such individuals but it may be helpful to form links with local academic institutions where there is likely to be a concentration of published researchers.

In total, we hope we have given a strong case for evaluation. Good evaluation is in everyone's best interest: the client who participates in an effective programme; the practitioner whose practice should improve and become even more effective; and the wider practitioner community who benefit from learning from outcome studies.

References

Allsop, B. & Saunders, S. (1989). Relapse and alcohol problems. In M. Gossop (Ed.). *Relapse and Addictive Behaviour.* London: Tavistock/Routledge.

Annis, H. M. (1982). *Inventory of Drinking Situations (IDS-100).* Toronto, Canada: Addiction Research Foundation of Ontario.

Annis, H. M. (1987). *Situational Confidence Questionnaire (SCQ-39).* Toronto, Canada: Addiction Research Foundation of Ontario.

Annis, H. M. (1990). Relapse to substance abuse: Empirical findings within a cognitive-social learning approach. *Journal of Psychoactive Drugs*, 22, 117–24.

Annis, H. M. & Davis, C. S. (1989). Relapse prevention. In R. K. Hester & W. R. Miller (Eds). *Handbook of Alcoholism Treatment Approaches.* New York: Pergamon Press.

Argyle, M. (1967). *The Psychology of Interpersonal Behaviour.* Harmondsworth: Penguin.

Argyle, M. (1975). *Bodily Communication.* London: Methuen.

Argyle, M. (1983). *The Psychology of Interpersonal Behaviour.* (4th edn). Harmondsworth: Penguin.

Argyle, M. (1986). Social skills and the analysis of situations and conversations. In C. R. Hollin & P. Trower (Eds). *Handbook of Social Skills Training: Clinical Applications and New Dimensions.* Vol. 2. Oxford: Pergamon Press.

Argyle, M. & Kendon, A. (1967). The experimental analysis of social performance. In L. Berkowitz (Ed.). *Advances in Experimental Social Psychology.* Vol. 3. New York: Academic Press.

Armor, D. J., Polich, J. M. & Stambul, H. B. (1976). *Alcoholism and Treatment.* Santa Monica: Rand Corporation.

Armor, D. J., Polich, J. M. & Stambul, H. B. (1978). *Alcoholism and Treatment.* New York: Wiley.

Ashmore, Z. & Jarvie, J. (1987). Job skills for young offenders. In B. J. McGurk, D. M. Thornton & M. Williams (Eds). *Applying Psychology to Imprisonment: Theory and Practice.* London: HMSO.

Babor, T. F., Stephens, R. S. & Marlatt, G. A. (1987). Verbal report methods in clinical research on alcoholism: Response bias and its minimization. *Journal of Studies on Alcohol*, 48, 410–24.

Bandura, A. (1977a). *Social Learning Theory.* New York: Prentice Hall.

Bandura, A. (1977b). Self-efficacy: Towards a unifying theory of behavioral change. *Psychological Review*, 84, 191–215.

Bandura, A. (1986). *Social Foundations of Thought and Action: A Social Cognitive Theory.* Englewood Cliffs, NJ: Prentice-Hall.

Barlow, D. H. & Hersen, M. (1984). *Single Case Experimental Designs:*

Strategies for Studying Behavior Change (2nd edn). New York: Pergamon Press.

Barrera, M., Rosen, G. M. & Glasgow, R. E. (1981). Rights, risks, and responsibilities in the use of self-help psychotherapy. In G. T. Hannah, W. P. Christian & H. B. Clark (Eds). *Preservation of Client Rights*. New York: The Free Press.

Becker, R. E. & Heimberg, R. G. (1988). Assessment of social skills. In A. S. Bellack & M. Hersen (Eds). *Behavioral Assessment: A Practical Handbook* (3rd edn). New York: Pergamon Press.

Bensley, L. S. & Wu, R. (1991). The role of psychological reactance in drinking following alcohol prevention messages. *Journal of Applied Social Psychology*, 24, 1111–24.

Borrill, J. A., Rosen, B. K. & Summerfield, A. B. (1987). The influence of alcohol on judgement of facial expressions of emotion. *British Journal of Medical Psychology*, 60, 71–77.

Braucht, G. N., Brakarsh, D., Folungstad, D. & Berry, K. L. (1973). Deviant drug use in adolescence. *Psychological Bulletin*, 79, 92–106.

Brewin, C. (1988). *Cognitive Foundations of Clinical Psychology*. London: Lawrence Erlbaum.

Brophy, J. (1981). Teacher praise: A functional analysis. *Review of Educational Research*, 51, 5–32.

Brown, M. (1982). Maintenance and generalization issues on skills training with chronic schizophrenics. In J. P. Curran & P. M. Monti (Eds). *Social Skills Training: A Practice Handbook for Assessment and Treatment*. New York: The Guilford Press.

Brown, S. A. (1989). Life events of adolescents in relation to personal and parental substance abuse. *American Journal of Psychiatry*, 146, 484–9.

Brown, S. A. & Stetson, B. A. (1988). Coping with drinking pressures: Adolescent versus parent perspectives. *Adolescence*, 23, 297–301.

Brown, W. C. (1961). *Freud and the Post-Freudians*. Harmondsworth: Penguin.

Caddy, G. R., Addington, H. J. & Perkins, D. (1978). Individualized behavior therapy for alcoholics: A third year independent double-blind follow-up. *Behavior Research and Therapy*, 16, 345–62.

Catania, A. C. & Harnad, S. (1988). *The Selection of Behavior: The Operant Behaviorism of B. F. Skinner: Comments and Consequences*. Cambridge: Cambridge University Press.

Chaney, E. F. (1989). Social skills training. In R. K. Hester & W. R. Miller (Eds). *Handbook of Alcoholism Treatment Approaches*. New York: Pergamon.

Chaney, E. F., O'Leary, M. R. & Marlatt, G. A. (1978). Skill training with alcoholics. *Journal of Consulting and Clinical Psychology*, 46, 1092–104.

Chick, J., Lloyd, G. & Crombie, E. (1985). Counselling problem drinkers in medical wards: A controlled study. *British Medical Journal*, 290, 965–7.

Clinebell, H. (1984). *Basic Types of Pastoral Care and Counselling*. London: SCM Press.

Collins, J. J. (Ed.). (1982) *Drinking and Crime*. London: Tavistock Publications.

Committee to Identify Research Opportunities in the Prevention and Treatment of Alcohol-Related Problems (1992). Prevention and treatment of alcohol-related problems: Research opportunities. *Journal of Studies on Alcohol*, 53, 5–16.

Coulthard, M. (1984). Conversation analysis and social skills training. In P. Trower (Ed.). *Radical Approaches to Social Skills Training*. London: Croom Helm.

Davidson, R. (1987). Assessment of the alcohol dependence syndrome: A review of self-report screening questionnaires. *British Journal of Clinical Psychology*, **26**, 243—55.

Davidson, R. & Raistrick, D. (1986). The validity of the Short Alcohol Dependence Data (SADD) Questionnaire. *British Journal of Addiction*, **81**, 217—22.

Davies, D. L. (1962). Normal drinking in recovered alcoholics. *Quarterly Journal of Studies on Alcohol*, **23**, 94—104.

Dielman, T. E., Shope, J. T., Butchart, A. T. & Campanelli, P. C. (1986). Prevention of adolescent alcohol misuse: An elementary school programme. *Journal of Pediatric Psychology*, **11**, 259—81.

Donovan, D. M. (1988). Assessment of addictive behaviors: Implications of an emerging biopsychosocial model. In D. M. Donovan & G. A. Marlatt (Eds). *Assessment of Addictive Behaviors*. New York: Hutchinson.

Donovan, J. E., Jessor, R. & Costa, F. M. (1991). Adolescent health behavior and conventionality—unconventionality: An extension of problem-behavior theory. *Health Psychology*, **10**, 52—61.

D'Zurilla, T. J. & Goldfried, M. R. (1971). Problem solving and behavior modification. *Journal of Abnormal Psychology*, **78**, 107—26.

D'Zurilla, T. J. & Nezu, A. (1982). Social problem solving in adults. *Advances in Cognitive-Behavioral Research and Therapy*, Vol. 1. New York: Academic Press.

Editorial (1989). Health care for children and adolescents in detention centers, jails, lock-ups, and other court-sponsored residential facilities. *Pediatrics*, **84**, 1118—20.

Edwards, G. (1987). *The Treatment of Drinking Problems*. Oxford: Blackwell Scientific Publications.

Edwards, G., Orford, J., Egert, S., Guthrie, S., Hawker, A., Hensman, C., Mitcheson, M., Oppenheimer, E. & Taylor, C. (1977). Alcoholism: A controlled trial of "treatment" and "advice". *Journal of Studies on Alcohol*, **38**, 1004—31.

Farrington, D. P. (1983). Offending from 10 to 25 years of age. In K. Teilmann van Dusen & S. A. Mednick (Eds). *Prospective Studies of Crime and Delinquency*. The Hague: Kluwer Nijnoff.

Farrington, D. P. (1986). Age and crime. In M. Tonny & N. Morris (Eds). *Crime and Justice: An Annual Review of Research* (Vol. 7). Chicago: University of Chicago Press.

Farrington, D. P. (1987). Epidemiology. In H. C. Quay (Ed.). *Handbook of Juvenile Delinquency*. New York: Wiley.

Farrington, D. P. & West, D. J. (1990). The Cambridge study in delinquent development: A long-term follow-up of 411 London males. In H. J. Kerner & G. Kaiser (Eds). *Criminality: Personality, Behaviour and Life History*. Berlin: Springer-Verlag.

Fingarette, H. (1989). *Heavy Drinking: The Myth of Alcoholism as a Disease*. Berkeley: University of California Press.

Fishman, D. B., Rotgers, F. & Franks, C. M. (Eds) (1988). *Paradigms in Behavior Therapy: Present and Promise*. New York: Springer.

Frank, S. J., Jacobson, S. & Tuer, M. (1990). Psychological predictors of young adults' drinking behaviors. *Journal of Personality and Social Psychology*, **59**, 770—80.

Freedman, B. J., Rosenthal, L., Donahue, C. P., Schlondt, D. G. & McFall, R. M. (1978). A social-behavioral analysis of skill deficits in delinquent and non-delinquent adolescent boys. *Journal of Consulting and Clinical Psychology*, **46**, 1448—62.

Fuller, J. R. (1979). Alcohol abuse and the treatment of young offenders. *Directorate of Psychological Services Report*, Series 1, No. 13. London: Home Office.

Furnham, A. & Argyle, M. (1981). The theory, practice, and application of social skills training. *International Journal of Behavioural Social Work and Abstracts*, **1**, 125—43.

Glasser, W. (1976). *Positive Addictions*. New York: Harper Row.

Glatt, M. M. & Mills, D. R. (1968). Alcohol abuse and alcoholism in the young. *British Journal of Addiction*, **63**, 183—90.

Goddard, E. & Ikin, C. (1989). *Drinking in England and Wales in 1987*. Office of Population Censuses and Surveys: Social Survey Division. London: HMSO.

Good, D. (1986). Social skills and the analysis of conversation. In C. R. Hollin & P. Trower (Eds). *Handbook of Social Skills Training: Clinical Applications and New Directions*. Vol. 2. Oxford: Pergamon Press.

Guze, S. B., Tuason, V. B., Stewart, M. A. & Picken, B. (1963). The drinking history: A comparison of reports by subjects and their relatives. *Quarterly Journal of Studies on Alcohol*, **24**, 249—60.

Hall, S. M., Loeb, P., Coyne, K. & Cooper, J. (1981). Increasing employment in ex-heroin addicts I: Criminal justice sample. *Behavior Therapy*, **12**, 453—60.

Hargie, O., Saunders, C. & Dickson, D. (1981). *Social Skills in Interpersonal Communication*. London: Croom Helm.

Hayes, S. C. (Ed.) (1989). *Rule-Governed Behavior: Cognition, Contingencies and Instructional Control*. New York: Plenum Press.

Heather, N. (1981). Relationship between delinquency and drunkenness among Scottish young offenders. *British Journal on Alcohol and Alcoholism*, **16**, 50—61.

Heather, N. (1982). Alcohol dependence and problem drinking in Scottish young offenders. *British Journal on Alcohol and Alcoholism*, **17**, 145—54.

Heather, N. (1989). Brief intervention strategies. In R. K. Hester & W. R. Miller (Eds). *Handbook of Alcoholism Treatment Approaches*. New York: Pergamon.

Heather, N. & Bradley, B. P. (1990). Cue exposure as a practical treatment for addictive disorders: Why are we waiting? *Addictive Behaviors*, **15**, 335—37.

Heather, N., Gold, R. & Rollnick, S. (1991). *Readiness to Change Questionnaire: User's Manual*. National Drug and Alcohol Research Centre, Technical Report No. 15.

Heather, N., Kissoon-Singh, J. & Fenton, G. W. (1990). Assisted natural recovery from alcohol problems: Effects of a self-help manual with and without supplementary telephone contact. *British Journal of Addiction*, **85**, 1177—85.

Heather, N. & Robertson, I. (1981). *Controlled Drinking*. London: Methuen.

Heather, N. & Robertson, I. (1985). *Problem Drinking: The New Approach*. Harmondsworth: Penguin.

Heather, N., Robertson, I., McPherson, B., Allsop, S. & Fulton, A. (1987) Effectiveness of a controlled drinking self-help manual: one year follow-up results. *British Journal of Clinical Psychology*, **26**, 279–87.

Heather, N., Whitton, B. & Robertson, I. (1986). Evaluation of a self-help manual for media-recruited problem drinkers: Six-month follow-up results. *British Journal of Clinical Psychology*, **25**, 19–34.

Henderson, M. & Hollin, C. R. (1986). Social skills training and delinquency. In C. R. Hollin & P. Trower (Eds). *Handbook of Social Skills Training. Volume 1: Applications Across the Life Span*. Oxford: Pergamon Press.

Herbert, M. (1987). *Conduct Disorders of Childhood and Adolescence*. Chichester: Wiley.

Herbert, M. (1990). *Planning a Research Project: A Guide for Practitioners and Trainees in the Helping Professions*. London: Cassell.

Hester, R. K. & Miller, W. R. (1987). Self-control training. In H. T. Blane & K. E. Leonard (Eds). *Psychological Theories of Drinking and Alcoholism*. New York: The Guilford Press.

Hodgson, R. (1989). Resisting temptation: A psychological analysis. *British Journal of Addiction*, **84**, 251–7.

Hoffman, N. G., Ninonuevo, F., Mozey, J. & Luxenberg, M. G. (1987). Comparison of court-referred DWI arrestees with other outpatients in substance abuse treatment. *Journal of Studies on Alcohol*, **48**, 591–4.

Hollin, C. R. (1983). Young offenders and alcohol: A survey of the drinking behaviour of a Borstal population. *Journal of Adolescence*, **6**, 161–74.

Hollin, C. R. (1989). *Psychology and Crime: An Introduction to Criminological Psychology*. London: Routledge.

Hollin, C. R. (1990). Social skills training with delinquents: A look at the evidence and some recommendations for practice. *British Journal of Social Work*, **20**, 483–93.

Hollin, C. R. & Henderson, M. (1984). Social skills training with young offenders: False expectations and failure of training. *Behavioural Psychotherapy*, **12**, 331–41.

Hollin, C. R. & Trower, P. (Eds) (1986a). *Handbook of Social Skills Training. Vol. 1: Applications Across the Life Span*. Oxford: Pergamon.

Hollin, C. R. & Trower, P. (Eds) (1986b). *Handbook of Social Skills Training. Vol. 2: Clinical Applications and New Directions*. Oxford: Pergamon.

Hollin, C. R. & Trower, P. (1988). Development and applications of social skills training: A review and critique. In M. Hersen, R. M. Eisler & P. M. Miller (Eds). *Progress in Behavior Modification*. (Vol. 22). Beverly Hills, Ca: Sage Publications.

Home Office (1987). *Report of the Working Group on Young People and Alcohol*. London: Home Office.

Hope, T. (1985). Drinking and disorder in the inner city. In *Implementing Crime Prevention Measures*. Home Office Research Study, No. 86. London: HMSO.

Hopkins, R. H., Mauss, A. L., Kearney, K. A. & Weisheit, R. A. (1988). Comprehensive evaluation of a model alcohol education curriculum. *Journal of Studies on Alcohol*, **49**, 38–50.

Huff, G. (1987). Social skills training. In B. J. McGurk, D. M. Thornton & M. Williams (Eds). *Applying Psychology to Imprisonment: Theory and Practice*. London: HMSO.

Hull, J. G. & Schnurr, P. P. (1986). The role of self in alcohol use. In L. M.

Hartman & K. R. Blankstein (Eds). *Perception of Self in Emotional Disorder and Psychotherapy*. New York: Plenum Press.

Jacobson, E. (1929). Progressive Relaxation. Chicago: University of Chicago Press.

Jellinek, E. M. (1960). *The Disease Concept of Alcoholism*. New Haven, Connecticut: Hillhouse Press.

Jessor, R. & Jessor, R. L. (1975). Adolescent development and the onset of drinking. *Journal of Studies on Alcohol*, **36**, 419–39.

Kanfer, F. H. & Gaelick, L. (1986). Self-management methods. In F. H. Kanfer & A. P. Goldstein (Eds). *Helping People Change: A Textbook of Methods*. New York: Pergamon Press.

Kazdin, A. E. (1979). Fictions, factions, and functions of behavior therapy. *Behavior Therapy*, **10**, 629–54.

Kinder, B. N., Pape, N. E. & Walfish, S. (1980). Drug and alcohol education programs: A review of outcome studies. *The International Journal of the Addictions*, **15**, 1035–54.

Kline, P. (1984). *Psychology and Freudian Theory*. London: Methuen.

Knapp, M. L. (1978). *Non-Verbal Communication in Human Interaction*. New York: Holt, Rinehart and Winston.

Laberg, J. C. (1990). What is presented, and what prevented, in cue exposure and response prevention with alcohol dependent subjects. *Addictive Behaviors*, **15**, 367–86.

Lamal, P.A. (Ed.) (1991). *Behavioral Analysis of Societies and Cultural Practices*. New York: Hemisphere.

Larimer, M. E. & Marlatt, G. A. (1990). Applications of relapse prevention with moderation goals. *Journal of Psychoactive Drugs*, **22**, 189–95.

Laws, D. R. (Ed.) (1989). *Relapse Prevention with Sex Offenders*. New York: The Guilford Press.

Lazarus, R. S. & Cohen, J. B. (1977). Environmental stress. In I. Altman & J. F. Wohlwill (Eds). *Human Behavior and the Environment: Current Theory and Research*, Vol. 2. New York: Plenum Press.

Lee, V. L. (1988). *Beyond Behaviorism*. Hillside, New Jersey: Lawrence Erlbaum.

Leigh, G. & Skinner, H. A. (1988). Physiological assessment. In D. M. Donovan & G. A. Marlatt (Eds). *Assessment of Addictive Behaviours*. London: Hutchinson.

Levine, J. & Zeigler, E. (1973). The essential-reactive distinction in alcoholism: A developmental approach. *Journal of Abnormal Psychology*, **81**, 242–9.

Lowe, C. F. (1983). Radical behaviourism and human psychology. In G. C. L. Davey (Ed.). *Animal Models of Human Behavior*. Chichester: Wiley.

Mahoney, M. J. & Thoresen, C. E. (1974). *Self-Control: Power to the Person*. Monterey, Ca: Brookes/Cole.

Marlatt, G. A. (1985a). Relapse prevention: Theoretical rationale and overview of the model. In G. A. Marlatt & J. R. Gordon (Eds). *Relapse Prevention*. New York: The Guilford Press.

Marlatt, G. A. (1985b). Situational determinants of relapse and skill-training interventions. In G. A. Marlatt & J. R. Gordon (Eds). *Relapse Prevention*. New York: The Guilford Press.

Marlatt, G. A. (1985c). Cognitive assessment and intervention procedures. In G. A. Marlatt & J. R. Gordon (Eds). *Relapse Prevention*. New York: The Guilford Press.

Marlatt, G. A. (1985d). Lifestyle modification. In G. A. Marlatt & J. R. Gordon (Eds). *Relapse Prevention*. New York: The Guilford Press.

Marlatt, G. A. (1990). Cue exposure and relapse prevention in the treatment of addictive behaviors. *Addictive Behaviors*, **15**, 395—9.

Marlatt, G. A., Demming, B. & Reid, J. B. (1973). Loss of control drinking in alcoholics: An experimental analogue. *Journal of Abnormal Psychology*, **81**, 233—41.

Marlatt, G. A. & George, W. H. (1984). Relapse prevention: Introduction and overview of the model. *British Journal of Addiction*, **79**, 261—73.

Marques, J. K. & Nelson, C. (1989). Understanding and preventing relapse in sex offenders. In M. Gossop (Ed.). *Relapse and Addictive Behaviour*. London: Tavistock/Routledge.

Marsh, A., Dobbs, J. & White, A. (1986). *Adolescent Drinking*. Office of Population Censuses and Surveys; Social Survey Division. London: HMSO

Mauss, A. L., Hopkins, R. H., Weisheit, R. A. & Kearney, K. A. (1988). The problematic prospects for prevention in the classroom: Should alcohol education programs be expected to reduce drinking by youth? *Journal of Studies on Alcohol*, **49**, 51—61.

McConnaughy, E. A., DiClemente, C. C., Prochaska, J. O. & Velicer, W. F. (1989). Stages of change in psychotherapy: A follow-up report. *Psychotherapy*, **26**, 494—503.

McConnaughy, E. A., Prochaska, J. O. & Velicer, W. F. (1983). Stages of change in psychotherapy: Measurement and sample profiles. *Psychotherapy*, **20**, 368—75.

McCown, W., Johnson, J. & Austin, S. (1986). Inability of delinquents to recognise facial affects. *Journal of Social Behavior and Personality*, **1**, 489—96.

McDougall, C. & Boddis, S. (1991). Discrimination between anger and aggression: Implications for treatment. *Issues in Criminological and Legal Psychology No. 17*. Leicester: The British Psychological Society.

McGuire, J. & Priestley, P. (1985). *Offending Behaviour: Skills and Stratagems for Going Straight*. London: Batsford.

McMurran, M. (1991a). Young offenders and alcohol-related crime: What interventions will address the issues? *Journal of Adolescence*, **14**, 245—53.

McMurran, M. (1991b). A cognitive-behavioural intervention with a sex offender. *Delinquencia*, **2**, 311—30.

McMurran, M. & Baldwin, S. (1989). Services for prisoners with alcohol-related problems: A survey of UK prisons. *British Journal of Addiction*, **84**, 1053—8.

McMurran, M. & Baldwin, S. (1990). Evaluation: A practitioner's guide. In S. Baldwin (Ed.). *Alcohol Education and Offenders*. London: Batsford.

McMurran, M. & Hollin, C.R. (1989a). Drinking and delinquency: Another look at young offenders and their drinking. *British Journal of Criminology*, **29**, 386—94.

McMurran, M. & Hollin, C. R. (1989b). The Short Alcohol Dependence Data (SADD) Questionnaire: Norms and reliability data for male young offenders. *British Journal of Addiction*, **84**, 315—18.

McMurran, M., Hollin, C.R. & Bowen, A. (1990). Consistency of alcohol self-report measures in a male young offender population. *British Journal of Addiction*, **85**, 205—8.

McMurran, M. & Thomas, G. (1991). An intervention for alcohol-related offending. *Senior Nurse*, 11, 33—6.

McMurran, M. & Whitman, J. (1990). Strategies of self-control in male young offenders who have reduced their alcohol consumption without formal intervention. *Journal of Adolescence*, 13, 115—28.

Merry, J. (1966). The "loss of control" myth. *Lancet*, 4, 1257—8.

Midanik, L.T. (1982). The validity of self-reported alcohol consumption and alcohol problems: A literature review. *British Journal of Addiction*, 77, 357—82.

Midanik, L. T. (1988). Validity of self-reported alcohol use: A literature review and assessment. *British Journal of Addiction*, 83, 1019—29.

Miller, W. R. (1978). Behavioral treatment of problem drinkers: A comparative outcome study of three controlled drinking therapies. *Journal of Consulting and Clinical Psychology*, 46, 74—86.

Miller, W. R. (1983a). Controlled drinking: A history and critical review. *Journal of Studies on Alcohol*, 44, 68—83.

Miller, W. R. (1983b). Motivational interviewing with problem drinkers. *Behavioural Psychotherapy*, 11, 147—72.

Miller, W. R. (1985). Motivational interviewing: A review with special emphasis on alcoholism. *Psychological Bulletin*, 98, 84—107.

Miller, W. R. (1989). Matching individuals with interventions. In R. K. Hester & W. R. Miller (Eds). *Handbook of Alcoholism Treatment Approaches*. New York: Pergamon.

Miller, W. R. & Baca, L. M. (1983). Two-year follow-up of bibliotherapy and therapist directed controlled drinking training for problem drinkers. *Behavior Therapy*, 14, 441—8.

Miller, W. R., Gribskov, C. J. & Mortell, R. L. (1981). Effectiveness of a self-control manual for problem drinkers with and without therapist contact. *International Journal of the Addictions*, 16, 1247—54.

Miller, W. R. & Hester, R. K. (1986a). The effectiveness of alcohol treatment: What research reveals. In W. R. Miller & N. Heather (Eds). *Treating Addictive Behaviors: Processes of Change*. New York: Plenum Press.

Miller, W. R. & Hester, R. K. (1986b). Matching problem drinkers with optimal treatments. In W. R. Miller & N. Heather (Eds). *Treating Addictive Behaviors: Processes of Change*. New York: Plenum Press.

Miller, W. R. & Hester, R. K. (1987). Treating alcohol problems: Toward an informed eclecticism. In H. T. Blane & K. E. Leonard (Eds). *Psychological Theories of Drinking and Alcoholism*. New York: The Guilford Press.

Miller, W. R., Pechachek, T. F. & Hamburg, S. (1981). Group behavior therapy for problem drinkers. *International Journal of the Addictions*, 16, 829—39.

Miller, W. R. & Rollnick, S. (1991). *Motivational Interviewing: Preparing People to Change*. New York: The Guilford Press.

Miller, W. R. & Sovereign, R. G. (1989). The Check-up: A model for early intervention in addictive behaviors. In T. Loberg, W. R. Miller, P. E. Nathan & G. A. Marlatt (Eds). *Addictive Behaviors: Prevention and Early Intervention*. Amsterdam: Swets and Zeitlinger.

Miller, W. R., Sovereign, R. G. & Krege, B. (1988). Motivational interviewing with problem drinkers: II The drinker's check-up as a preventive intervention. *Behavioural Psychotherapy*, 16, 251—68.

Miller, W. R. & Taylor, C. A. (1980). Relative effectiveness of bibliotherapy, individual, and group self-control training in the treatment of problem drinkers. *Addictive Behaviors*, **5**, 13—24.

Modgil, S. & Modgil, C. (1987). *B. F. Skinner: Consensus and Controversy.* New York: Falmer Press.

Monti, P. M., Abrams, D. B., Binkoff, J. A. & Zwick, W. R. (1986). Social skills training and substance abuse. In C. R. Hollin & P. Trower (Eds). *Handbook of Social Skills Training, Vol. 2: Clinical Applications and New Directions.* Oxford: Pergamon Press.

Monti, P. M., Abrams, D. B., Kadden, R. M. & Cooney, N. L. (1989). *Treating Alcohol Dependence.* London: Cassell.

Murdoch, D., Pihl, R. O. & Ross, D. (1990). Alcohol and crimes of violence: Present issues. *The International Journal of the Addictions*, **25**, 1065—81.

Murray, D. M. & Perry, C. L. (1987). The measurement of substance use among adolescents: When is the "bogus pipeline" method needed? *Addictive Behaviors*, **12**, 225—33.

Myers. T. (1983). Corroboration of self-reported alcohol consumption: A comparison of the accounts of a group of male prisoners and those of their wives/cohabitees. *Alcohol and Alcoholism*, **18**, 67—74.

Ogborne, A. C. & Glaser, F. B. (1981). Characteristics of affiliates of Alcoholics Anonymous: A review of the literature. *Journal of Studies on Alcohol*, **39**, 1297—8.

Orford, J. & Keddie, A. (1986). Abstinence or controlled drinking in clinical practice: A test of the dependence and persuasion hypothesis. *British Journal of Addiction*, **81**, 495—504.

Orford, J. & Velleman, R. (1991). The environmental intergenerational transmission of alcohol problems: A comparison of two hypotheses. *British Journal of Medical Psychology*, **64**, 189—200.

Osborn, A. F. (1963). *Applied Imagination: Principles and Procedures of Creative Problem-Solving.* New York: Scribner.

Papandreou, N., Brooksbank, J. V. & McLaughlin, K. M. (1985). Alcohol and offending: A probation service's education programme. *Australian and New Zealand Journal of Criminology*, **18**, 67—72.

Perri, M. G. (1985). Self-change strategies for the control of smoking, obesity, and problem drinking. In S. Shiffman & T. A. Wills (Eds) *Coping and Substance Use.* London: Academic Press.

Pithers, W. D., Marques, J. K., Gibat, C. C. & Marlatt, G. A. (1983). Relapse prevention with sexual aggressives: A self-control model of treatment and maintenance of change. In J. G. Greer & I. R. Stuart (Eds). *The Sexual Aggressor: Current Perspectives on Treatment.* New York: Van Nostrand.

Prochaska, J. O. & DiClemente, C. C. (1986). Toward a comprehensive model of change. In W. R. Miller & N. Heather (Eds). *Treating Addictive Behaviors: Processes of Change.* New York: Plenum Press.

Raistrick, D. S., Dunbar, G. & Davidson, R. J. (1983). Development of a questionnaire to measure alcohol dependence. *British Journal of Addiction*, **78**, 89—95.

Ramsay, M. (1982). *City Centre Crime: The Scope for Situational Prevention.* Research and Planning Unit Paper, No. 10. London: Home Office.

Rankin, H., Hodgson, R. & Stockwell, T. (1980). The behavioural measurement of dependence. *British Journal of Addiction*, **75**, 43—7.

Rankin, H., Hodgson, R. & Stockwell, T. (1983). Cue exposure and response prevention with alcoholics: A controlled trial. *Behavior Research and Therapy*, **21**, 435—46.

Rescorla, R. A. (1988). Pavlovian conditioning: It's not what you think it is. *American Psychologist*, **43**, 151—60.

Riley, D. (1987). Time and crime: The link between teenager lifestyle and delinquency. *Journal of Quantitative Criminology*, **3**, 339—54.

Robertson, I. & Heather, N. (1986). *Let's Drink To Your Health!* Leicester: The British Psychological Society.

Robinson, D., Grossman, M. & Porporino, F. (1991). *Effectiveness of the Cognitive Skills Training Program: From Pilot to National Implementation*. Ottawa: Correctional Service of Canada.

Rogers, C. R. (1973). The interpersonal relationship: The core of guidance. In C. R. Rogers & B. Stevens (Eds). *Person to Person: The Problem of Being Human*. London: Souvenir Press.

Rohsenow, D. J., Smith, R. E. & Johnson, J. (1986). Stress management as a prevention program for heavy social drinkers. *Addictive Behaviors*, **10**, 45—54.

Rollnick, S., Heather, N., Gold, R. & Hall, W. (1992). Development of a short "readiness to change" questionnaire for use in brief opportunistic interventions among excessive drinkers. *British Journal of Addiction*, **87**, 743—54.

Ross, R. R., Fabiano, E. A. & Ross, R. D. (1986). *Reasoning and Rehabilitation*. Ottawa: University of Ottawa.

Ross, R. R. & Lightfoot, L. O. (1985). *Treatment of the Alcohol-Abusing Offender*. Springfield, Il: C. C. Thomas.

Royal College of Physicians (1987). *The Medical Consequences of Alcohol Abuse: A Great and Growing Evil*. London: Tavistock Publications.

Rundall, T. G. & Bruvold, W. H. (1988). A meta-analysis of school-based smoking and alcohol use prevention programs. *Health Education Quarterly*, **15**, 317—34.

Rutter, M. & Giller, H. (1983). *Juvenile Delinquency: Trends and Perspectives*. Harmondsworth: Penguin.

Saunders, B. & Allsop, S. (1989). Relapse: A critique. In M. Gossop (Ed.). *Relapse and Addictive Behaviour*. London: Tavistock/Routledge.

Savage, S. A., Hollin, C. R. & Hayward, A. J. (1990). Self-help manuals for problem drinking: The relative effectiveness of their educational and therapeutic components. *British Journal of Clinical Psychology*, **29**, 373—82.

Serna, L. A., Schumaker, J. B., Hazel, J. S. & Sheldon, J. B. (1986). Teaching reciprocal social skills to delinquents and their parents. *Journal of Clinical Child Psychology*, **15**, 64—77.

Shiffman, S. (1989). Conceptual issues in the study of relapse. In M. Gossop (Ed.). *Relapse and Addictive Behaviour*. London: Tavistock/ Routledge.

Shiffman, S., Read, L., Maltese, J., Rapkin, D. & Jarvik, M. E. (1985). Preventing relapse in ex-smokers: A self-management approach. In G. A. Marlatt & J. Gordon (Eds). *Relapse Prevention*. New York: The Guilford Press.

Siegal, L. J. (1986). *Criminology* (2nd edn). St. Paul, Minnesota: West Publishing.

Singer, L. (1990). Evaluation of alcohol education courses. In S. Baldwin (Ed.). *Alcohol Education and Offenders*. London: Batsford.

Sisson, R. W. & Azrin, N. H. (1989). The Community Reinforcement

Approach. In R. K. Hester & W. R. Miller (Eds). *Handbook of Alcoholism Treatment Approaches*. New York: Pergamon.

Skinner, B. F. (1974). *About Behaviorism*. London: Cape.

Skinner, B. F. (1986a). What is wrong with daily life in the Western world? *American Psychologist*, **41**, 568–74.

Skinner, B. F. (1986b). Is it behaviorism? *Behavioral and Brain Sciences*, **9**, 716.

Sleap, H. (1977). *Problem drinkers at Glen Parva: A survey of the drinking habits and alcohol-related problems of a delinquent male population*. Unpublished manuscript, HM YOC Glen Parva, Leicester.

Smith, R. (1981). Preventing alcohol problems: A job for Canute? *British Medical Journal*, **283**, 972–5.

Sobell, M. B. & Sobell, L. C. (1973). Individualized behavior therapy for alcoholics. *Behavior Therapy*, **4**, 49–72.

Sobell, M. B. & Sobell, L. C. (1976). Second year treatment outcome of alcoholics treated by individualized behavior therapy: Results. *Behavior Research and Therapy*, **14**, 195–215.

Sobell, L. C., Sobell, M. B., Riley, D. M., Schuller, R., Pavan, D. S., Cancilla, A., Klajner, F. & Leo, G. I. (1988). The reliability of alcohol abusers' self-reports of drinking and life events that occurred in the distant past. *Journal of Studies on Alcohol*, **49**, 225–32.

Spence, S. H. (1981). Differences in social skills performance between institutionalized male offenders and a comparable group of boys without offence records. *British Journal of Clinical Psychology*, **20**, 163–71.

Stall, R. (1983). An examination of spontaneous remission from problem drinking in the Bluegrass region of Kentucky. *Journal of Drug Issues*, **13**, 191–206.

Stall, R. & Biernacki, P. (1986). Spontaneous remission from the problematic use of substances: An inductive model derived from a comparative analysis of the alcohol, opiate, tobacco, and food/obesity literature. *The International Journal of the Addictions*, **21**, 1–23.

Stallard, A. & Heather, N. (1989). Relapse prevention and AIDS among intravenous drug users. In M. Gossop (Ed.). *Relapse and Addictive Behaviour*. London: Tavistock/Routledge.

Sternberg, B. (1985). Relapse in weight control: Definitions, processes, and prevention. In G. A. Marlatt & J. Gordon (Eds). *Relapse Prevention*. New York: The Guilford Press.

Stuart, R. B. (1974). Teaching facts about drugs: Pushing or preventing? *Journal of Educational Psychology*, **66**, 189–201.

Sturgis, E. T., Calhoun, K. S. & Best, C. L. (1979). Correlates of assertive behavior in alcoholics. *Addictive Behaviors*, **4**, 193–7.

Sugarman, A. A., Reilly, D. & Albahar, R. S. (1965). Social competence and essential-reactive distinction in alcoholism. *Archives of General Psychiatry*, **12**, 552–6.

Swadi, H. (1988). Drug and substance abuse among 3,333 London adolescents. *British Journal of Addiction*, **83**, 935–42.

Swadi, H. & Zeitlin, H. (1988). Peer influence and adolescent substance abuse: A promising side? *British Journal of Addiction*, **83**, 153–7.

Temple, M. & Ladouceur, P. (1986). The alcohol-crime relationship as an age-specific phenomenon: A longitudinal study. *Contemporary Drug Problems*, **13**, 89–115.

Tether, P. & Robinson, D. (1986). *Preventing Local Problems: A Guide to Local Action*. London: Tavistock Publications.

Thorne, F. C. (1965). *The Sex Inventory*. Brandon, Vermont: Clinical Psychology Publishing Company.

Trower, P., Bryant, B. & Argyle, M. (1978). *Social Skills and Mental Health*. London: Methuen.

Tuchfeld, B. S. (1981). Spontaneous remission in alcoholics: Empirical observations and theoretical implications. *Journal of Studies on Alcohol*, 42, 626—41.

Velicer, W. F., DiClemente, C. C., Rossi, J. S. & Prochaska, J. O. (1990). Relapse situations and self-efficacy: An integrative model. *Addictive Behaviors*, 15, 271—83.

Veneziano, C. & Veneziano, L. (1988). Knowledge of social skills among institutionalized juvenile delinquents. *Criminal Justice and Behavior*, 15, 152—71.

Vogler, R. E., Compton, J. V. & Weissbach, T. A. (1976). The referral problem in the field of alcohol use. *Journal of Community Psychology*, 4, 357—61.

Vuchinich, R. E., Tucker, J. A. & Harllee, L. M. (1988). Behavioral assessment. In D. M. Donovan & G. A. Marlatt (Eds). *Assessment of Addictive Behaviors*. London: Hutchinson.

Ward, C. I. & McFall, R. M. (1986). Further validation of the problem inventory for adolescent girls: Comparing caucasians and black delinquents and non-delinquents. *Journal of Consulting and Clinical Psychology*, 54, 732—3.

Watson, C. G., Brown, K., Tilleskjor, C., Jacobs, L. & Pucel, J. (1988). The comparative recidivism rates of voluntary- and coerced-admission male alcoholics. *Journal of Clinical Psychology*, 44, 573—81.

Watson, J. B. (1913). Psychology as the behaviourist views it. *Psychological Review*, 20, 158—77.

Welte, J. W. & Miller, B. A. (1987). Alcohol use by violent and property offenders. *Drug and Alcohol Dependence*, 19, 313—24.

Werch, C. E., Gorman, D. R. & Marty, P. J. (1987). Relationship between alcohol consumption and alcohol problems in young adults. *Journal of Drug Education*, 17, 261—76.

West, D. J. (1982). *Delinquency: Its Roots. Careers and Prospects*. London: Heinemann.

West, D. J. & Farrington, D. P. (1977). *The Delinquent Way of Life*. London: Heinemann.

Wilkinson, J. & Canter, S. (1980). *Social Skills Training Manual: Assessment, Programme Design and Management of Training*. Chichester: Wiley.

Williams, G. (1975). The definition of crime. In J. Smith & B. Hogan (Eds). *Criminal Law*. (2nd edn). London: Butterworths.

Wilson, G. T. (1988). Alcohol and anxiety. *Behavior Research and Therapy*, 26, 369—81.

Wolfgang, M. E., Thorberry, T. P. & Figlio, R. M. (1987). *From Boy to Man. From Delinquency to Crime*. Chicago: University of Chicago Press.

Young, R. McD., Oei, T. P. S. & Knight, R. G. (1990). The tension-reduction hypothesis revisited. *British Journal of Addiction*, 85, 31—40.

Zuriff, G. E. (1985). *Behaviorism: A Conceptual Reconstruction*. New York: Columbia University Press.

List of Resources

ADDRESSES

Alcohol Concern
305 Grays Inn Road, London WC1X 8QF

Alcoholics Anonymous
PO Box 1, Stonebow House, Stonebow, York YO1 2NJ

Health Education Authority
Hamilton House, Mabledon Place, London WC1H 9TX

National Association for the Care & Resettlement of Offenders (NACRO)
169 Clapham Road, London SW9 0PU

Northern Ireland Council on Alcohol
40 Elmswood Avenue, Belfast BT9 6AZ

Scottish Council on Alcohol
137–145 Sauchiehall Street, Glasgow G2 4EW

The Advisory Council on Alcohol & Drug Education (TACADE)
1 Hulme Place, The Crescent, Salford, Manchester M5 4QA

SERVICES DIRECTORY

Alcohol Services Directory
Published for Alcohol Concern by:
Owen Wells Publisher, 23 Eaton Road, Ilkley LS29 9PU
ISBN 0-904553-24-8
£7.75

SELF-HELP MANUALS

Ian Robertson & Nick Heather (1986)
Let's Drink To Your Health!
The British Psychological Society, St Andrew's House, 48 Princess
Road East, Leicester LE1 7DR
ISBN 0-901715-60-3
£3.95

William R. Miller & Ricardo F. Munoz (1983)
How To Control Your Drinking
Sheldon Press, SPCK, Marylebone Road, London NW1 4DU
ISBN 0-85969-379-1
£5.95

RESEARCH JOURNALS

Alcohol

Alcohol & Alcoholism
American Journal of Drug & Alcohol Abuse
Addiction Research
Addictive Behaviors
British Journal of Addiction
Drug & Alcohol Dependence
Drug & Alcohol Review
International Journal of the Addictions
Journal of Alcohol & Drug Education
Journal of Drug Issues
Journal of Studies on Alcohol
Journal of Substance Abuse Treatment

Offenders

British Journal of Criminology
Crime and Delinquency
Criminal Behaviour & Mental Health
Criminology
Deviant Behavior
International Journal of Offender Therapy & Comparative
    Criminology
Journal of Interpersonal Violence

Journal of Offender Rehabilitation
Journal of Prison & Jail Health
Journal of Research in Crime & Delinquency
Medicine, Science & the Law
Psychology, Crime & Law

Adolescents

Adolescence
International Journal of Adolescence & Youth
Journal of Adolescence
Journal of Youth & Adolescence
Youth & Society

Index

Index compiled by A. C. Purton